# THE PIRELLI
## CALENDAR ALBUM

# THE PIRELLI CALENDAR ALBUM

## THE FIRST TWENTY-FIVE YEARS

Design by the Derek Forsyth Partnership Limited
Commentary by Michael Pye

Salem House Publishers
Topsfield, Massachusetts

*To the original supporters Guido Veronesi, continued support of Sandro Veronesi, enthusiasm
and backing and PR, Robert Newman, unrivalled help, PR, launch support, Tom Northey, our
agent Andrew Best, his wife Jackie Hunt for editorial help, Phil Beach the main
graphic designer and Mark A. Austin his assistant, Colin Webb our publisher and his staff, but
particularly Vivien Bowler, Lesley Davy for picture research, and Stephanie Keil for
editorial research, Christine Watkins for organising us, Geoff Dann our unfailing stills photographer,
all at Apex Photosetting and Paul Gilling for the artwork, but not forgetting
Doug Haywood for his moral support, and my wife Marisa for her faith. Many thanks – Derek.*

First published in the United States by
Salem House Publishers, 1988,
462 Boston Street, Topsfield, MA 01983.

Copyright in Photographs © Pirelli
Limited 1964, 1965, 1966, 1968, 1969,
1970, 1971, 1972, 1973, 1974, 1984,
1985, 1986, 1987, 1988.
Text Copyright © Michael Pye 1988
Design Copyright © The Derek Forsyth
Partnership Limited 1988

Designed by Phil Beach
Concept by Robert Newman

Library of Congress Cataloging in Publication Data

Pye, Michael, 1946 –
The Pirelli calendar album.

1. Popular culture – History – 20th century.
2. Great Britain – Popular culture – History – 20th century.
3. United States – Popular culture – History – 20th century.
4. Calendars.
I. Title.
CB430.P94 1988 909.82          87-35591

ISBN 0-88162-372-5

Archive material provided by the following libraries;
Topham Picture Library
Rex Features Ltd
Paul Popper Limited
BBC Hulton Picture Library
The Ronald Grant Archive

Colour separation by CLG, Verona
Printed and bound in Italy by Arnoldo Mondadori

# Preface By Derek Forsyth

The Pirelli calendars pose certain key creative questions. There were of course, and still are, many other calendars on which a great deal more money is spent by the promotors, and yet none has ever achieved the fame of Pirelli. Furthermore, these other calendars have often used the most famous models and photographers, and have been shot in even more exotic locations than were used for the Pirelli calendars, and yet Pirelli has always been the one great legend.

Why this pre-eminence? I think there have been a number of factors, perhaps the most important being a year-to-year awareness of the right note to strike for the ensuing months. For example, Sarah Moon's calendar represents a change of gear towards a gentle romanticism which turned out to be entirely relevant for its time. Again, to choose California and the Beach Boys by way of location in 1969 captured the prevailing mood. The photographers always had enormous talent and sense of style, but some were virtually unknown when they worked on the calendars. Perhaps fame is not always everything.

Then the models were often unusual in that they were chosen essentially for the people that they are, and their personalities were never subdued by artifice. The various elements that go to make up the Pirelli calendar – photographer, models, make-up and other artists – were all moulded by an art director to provide that unity of style which has been achieved year by year.

Perhaps the most important of all is Pirelli itself. The client has always seen the opportunities but has never interfered. First Guido Veronesi gave us a free hand and every support. His nephew Sandro Veronesi carries on the same tradition now. And Pirelli's PR activities, of which the calendar is only one part, are superbly imaginative and professional.

DEREK FORSYTH
1988

# 1

## THE PHENOMENON

*. . . it was only a friendly gesture –*
*a yearly present of dreams;*
*but Royals and Beatles and bullfighters*
*begged for it,*
*and even the Royal photographer*
*had to wait his turn . . .*

# The First Twenty-five Years

The usual men are in the London boardroom, middle-aged and in sober suits; mostly they talk about where to book the profits and how much the interim dividend should be, and how their main subsidiary is doing. They shuffle over their papers on the table, taut as rigging. But then they come to Item 8, which is Any Other Business, and they know that it really means: dreams.

The door opens and the public relations manager bustles in, with a stack of stiff white cards that he lays on the side table. The board are settling back expectantly. Every time they meet, they have to fret over currency movements, tyre sales, rubber prices; but once a year they have a privilege. They are the first to see the Pirelli Calendar.

Each white card holds an elegant picture of dancers, subtly bare, acting out the seasons – the brittle icicles of January, the hot abandon of July. *'Elegante,'* a director says, and *'Drammatica'*; this is an Italian company after all, 'Of course dancers aren't quite so – voluptuous, are they?' 'Ah,' says a senior Italian director, 'as you go upmarket there are always some disadvantages.' He is smiling wickedly. 'One year it is art, and the next year – we can make it more sexy.'

The directors sort through the pictures, looking for favourites. They know very well that these cards are a corporate asset, a guarantee of a glittering kind of goodwill for a company that makes rather practical, mundane goods – tyres, slippers, webbing. They have seen dozens of rival calendars over the years, with diving girls, teacher girls, Edwardian girls, brazen, Tahitian, even truck-driving girls; but nothing is quite like the Pirelli. It is a marketing triumph which almost overwhelmed the company, an institution so resilient it could even be reborn – a celebration that has lasted a quarter of a century.

Prince Philip and Prince Andrew gratefully acknowledge their copies; the Beatles sent a chauffeur for theirs; El Cordobes had it regularly, it made the Headmaster of Repton the envy of public school heads, and one Cabinet Minister made a private shrine for his copy inside a cupboard, to encourage him on bleak Whitehall days. When the calendar did not appear one year, rumour blamed its absence on Vatican disapproval. It was sold at Christie's, collected for the archive of the Tate Gallery, valued by insurance companies like fine art. Since very few were distributed, but much was said and written about them, they were hotly contested and defended. It was in a London cab that they were first called 'the world's greatest office status symbol,' by a newspaper editor fantasizing an excuse to publish the pictures on his centre spread; but the boast came true.

The calendar could never be bought, and only rarely begged; its exclusivity was planned and carefully maintained. At its peak, five full-time secretaries and six part-timers coped with the flood of requests and demands; *The Times* was littered with small advertisements to sell, buy or trade the Pirelli Calendar. The pleas were often ingenious – fathers for sons, 'schoolboys' with suspiciously mature writing on behalf of fathers; fiancées wanted it for fiancés who might otherwise stray, and diplomats for their contacts, although the un-named 'Representative of the Soviet Tobacco Industry' never did get one. The editors of *Farm Contractor* offered to swop their own calendar, with pictures of heavy agricultural machinery (their spokesman wrote: 'I do accept this offer is somewhat loaded . . .'). RAF officers from Strike Command had a suggestion, if all the calendars had gone: 'We do have an Instamatic camera – could you provide the girls?'

When the calendar was launched each year, some two hundred journalists would pack out the party, and the TV outside broadcast vans drew up outside; the hype was prodigious and carefully orchestrated. But it had more substance than that. Photographers thought of the Pirelli as an accolade; Norman Parkinson, famous for his fashion pictures and his Royal portraits, had to wait until 1985 for his chance. 'You couldn't be a photographer of international standing,' he says, 'unless you had done the Pirelli Calendar. But it was like Royal pictures – there are certain things in life you can't put yourself forward for. The more people know you want them, the less chance you've got.' It was an opportunity to take risks, to work for the ideal client. 'We work in a job where quite a high number of the things we manufacture are quite gruesomely dealt with,' the photographer Terence Donovan says. 'It's refreshing to see something handled with affection.'

In the Sixties, too, when lingerie models were thought slightly improper and 'glamour models' seemed to work in a quite separate trade, the Pirelli persuaded the most beautiful women to appear. Pat Booth, now a best-selling author (she is the tight brown belly under the sunflower in 1968) says: 'When the Pirelli came along, it became OK to take your clothes off. It made it respectable, because of the photographers.'

And yet the Pirelli Calendar was only a late variation on an old theme – girls to hang on the wall, like a thousand garage pin-ups, like the Leyland girls which the British truck firm produced from the 1940s or the Mintex calendar which in 1956 swathed Diana Dors in a sheet of lamé. Pirelli already had blotters, key rings, penknives and yellow dusters with their logo. But as a small company among the giants in the British tyre market they needed more than the acknowledged brilliance of their product. They needed friends.

The trial run, in 1963, now looks half-hearted. Donovan was the photographer; he was already a Kings Road chieftain, one of those East End boys who turned photography from sycophancy with a Leica into the star career of the Sixties. But even he could not make the pictures work; he remembers only the plainness of the girls and some talk of 'authenticity'. The idea – 'stupid, as it happens,' says Derek Forsyth, who was Pirelli's publicity head – was to take twelve export territories, show the product most sold in each, and a girl from each territory; the women were decor, irrelevant as potted palms.

The result now looks provincial. The 1963 calendar was less than a success; even the keyrings, with their out of register logo in a blur of red and black, seemed a better bet. But Derek Forsyth would not let the idea go. He had no money for national advertising, but he needed the attention of the dealers. The calendar would be a calling card for

Pirelli's salesmen. It was a friendly gesture, calculated to sell tyres.

The calendar's subject was women, but not the woman of the ordinary glamour shot with the red lips, fixed smile, huge breasts and meat-hook angles that said, very loudly in case you missed the point, 'sexy'. The Pirelli Calendar remade the rules for showing beautiful women. Glamour in the 1960s was the work of a single Soho photographer, Harrison Marks; it was indoor, retouched, heavy with mascara. Women were offered like chocolates on velvet; the make-up, pose and the physical exaggeration were all a kind of disguise. Imitators who lacked Marks' curiously stylized art made the flesh look dead. The pictures were exciting only because they broke taboos, showed or suggested what you were not supposed to see. They lost their power the first time a woman chose to show her breasts on a beach; glamour had to grow ruder.

Derek Forsyth made sure that the Pirelli pictures were very different, the women were to be individual and not anonymous – possible friends; you might (if very lucky) have dinner with one of them. Available is the wrong word, because they are not passively waiting for you to turn the page (and, by implication, set the price, as in those glamour pictures which dressed the girls like Soho tarts); but they are accessible. The pictures freeze a moment in their story; you can take it on where you want. Almost always, there is some sly element of wit as well, an unobvious detail or tension which will occupy a man's eye for a month.

To work, the pictures had to be stylish graphics, but they also had to be enticing; it was a tricky combination. When graphics are good, you admire the design, and stay on the surface. When an erotic image works, it seduces you into forgetting the boundaries of the picture, and entering its world. Derek Forsyth's calendar images had to work in the men's locker-room, but also be presentable in some outer office where secretaries passed; they had to be liked by the all-important dealer's wife who was so often the book-keeper and manager in the tyre business.

That contradiction kept the calendar alive; each year, it had to be resolved in a new way. But the board of directors and the mechanics in the locker-room found the pictures sometimes too hot and sometimes too innocuous. Derek Forsyth was the originator of the Pirelli phenomenon and art director for its first ten years. He always had thirteen slides to show the board, one of which they simply had to refuse – because of stray hairs, or some bit of anatomical detail; usually, they accepted the others. Still, some of his chosen pictures were re-cropped to make them less exact, and one was banned outright (it involved ice-cream). *The women were individual, not anonymous – possible friends; you might (if very lucky) have dinner with one . . . they are accessible.* While Pirelli did not want scandal, they did want attention, and sometimes the pressures were the other way. One senior executive had to be rebuked for wanting a stronger, raunchier 'fitter's version'; any pretension among the photographers was cut down by reminders of the 'garage' – the final arbiter of whether the calendar worked. The calendar was an annual high-wire act: it had to respond very exactly to the times – to style, to morals, to opinion.

The first of the great calendars, made for 1964, has the look of an album made by friends – an informal variation on some fashion shoot on a beach. The impact is in the smiles, not the flesh. There were no set rules for such a calendar, which was neither twelve advertising shots nor twelve air-brushed vixens; the photographers, often new to their craft, made up the rules as they went along. Even those sweet looks are new, acknowledging the camera and, by implication, the man holding it; they have nothing to do with glamour as forbidden information, glimpsed through a keyhole and maybe against the woman's will. These pictures are, subtly, about desire. They grew in years when London had very tentatively begun to 'swing', when anyone under thirty was busy improvising a social revolution and colour was beginning to seep into an anxious, black and white age (think of the stark graphic pages in chic magazines like *Town* and *Nova* and *Queen*, and the monochrome TV and the gritty, bitter movies – *A Taste of Honey, A Kind of Loving*). It was essential to be young, and the young were beginning to know it.

In 1967, the calendar did not appear: qualms, even rivalries within the group caused Pirelli to drop it. But when it burst back next year, it had become unstoppable. It drew on the hippified energy of the new generation, with its basement poets and its soulful songs and its zeal to let go and go thoroughly with the flow; it was flowers and love and expanding consciousness (considerably more legal in North Africa, the calendar's setting, than in Norbiton). The calendar lay on Californian beaches, watching the surf and listening to the Mamas and Papas, the Beach Boys; it caught the end of the simple European dream of America, before the war in Vietnam and in the streets of Chicago changed everything. And, as black-tie culture returned, and even the movies grew more interested in the rich and in class, in taking money for granted rather than making it, the calendar acquired its own kind of drama and glamour. It went away to a grand plantation house on a sunset island where skin tasted of heat and salt. The bodies were more bare, the abandon more emphatic.

Anything was possible on paper now, or so it seemed, but almost anything might offend. In the early 1970s feminism meant women's easy right to glory in their bodies, to go bare-breasted on the beach, but it also implied men's duty to realize what it meant when they stared. The Army took the pin-ups down from the barrack walls; the *Sun* ran the first pin-ups on Page Three. There was no consensus at all. The calendar had never taken its subject, which was woman, for granted; for 1972, a woman took its pictures. She brought languor and longing, something that blotted out the flat light and the careful detail of traditional glamour. She was followed by an artist playing elaborate games with the pin-up, and with the Vargas drawings in *Playboy*, the shine of rubber and leather in fetish drawings, and an underground of desire. And that was followed in 1974 by a calendar which again took women to a beach, somewhere far away (now that the jumbo jet was in service, a place had to be much further away to be exotic – the Seychelles, rather than Majorca). The formula might sound the same as the calendar's origins, but in ten years the inhibitions have faded away; in place of rules, there's an intimacy which is electric.

In 1974, just after that year's launch, the calendar was stopped. The reasons were cold and corporate – losses in Italy, losses in Britain, the need for cost-cutting; the mourning was fearful. But the name stayed strong enough to be brought back. Ten years later, just when Pirelli in Britain was at its lowest ebb, its managing director decided on a defiant course: to bring back the calendar as proof that Pirelli was here to stay. It was risky and brave.

The calendar of the Eighties was considered and premeditated, unlike the earlier ones; it was designed to do a marketing job, not

*These pictures are, subtly, about desire . . . The calendar became unstoppable . . . The bodies were more bare, the abandon more emphatic . . . There's an intimacy which is electric.*

just to make friends, and it added the product – the tread of a P6 tyre – to the sun and the sea and sand of the originals. It was full of wit and calculation, its story-telling pre-planned like a movie – backstage at a fashion show, where the girls are glorious between frocks; or in an artist's studio with the models; or using the real gold of jewellery against black skin, or dancers in motion. You could say that as desire began to seem more dangerous, the calendar turned cool; it was like a souvenir.

There's also a corporate change reflected among those glorious women. At the start, Pirelli was a company with panelled offices and three piece suits, a talent for throwing a generous, even riotous party at the Scottish Motor Show and knowing the dealers by name; but it was a small company among giants who sold their product on the strength of sharp prices rather than special qualities. The messy, marginal business of getting its name known was not half as important as a steady liaison with the garages, so it could be entrusted to young executives. 'Derek Forsyth used to go away with these seriously good looking women,' says Robert Newman, then public relations manager for Pirelli UK, 'and the managing director never knew when he was going to get back, and all he got was a bunch of colour transparencies. He had to have trust.'

Milan might object, but London refused to show the pictures in advance, or include a wheeled vehicle or stop the calendar dead; a subsidiary within an international group could be that autonomous. The Italian executives were proud of Pirelli's classic skyscraper in Milan, their links with the artists and photographers of Italy and their sponsorship of grand exhibitions – the works of Michelangelo, for example – which needed corporate money and political skills. They wondered about London – memos flew back and forth. They could also play on that thin but absolute façade of propriety which all Italians cultivate, the official strait-laces (think how *foreign* the life of Fellini's *La Dolce Vita* seemed to Romans); the Pirelli name should never go on a girlie calendar. Yet, almost every year it did.

It helped that Derek Forsyth and Robert Newman were (in their own words) 'a self-opinionated lot', cock-sure like any paid-up members of the younger generation battling with their elders in the

Sixties; but, Forsyth had also shown he knew how to sell the Pirelli Cinturato tyre, the kind of radial that appealed to sports car owners (small ads for a decade would offer Spitfires and Sprites, 'Cints fitted'). His methods were clever and oblique; there was often no car in the advertisements – a revolution for the trade. He was doing something the hierarchy did not quite understand, and it was working. They were not inclined to interfere.

The only problem was that the early calendars might look like a series of brilliant hunches; there was little marketing jargon or science to defend them when the tyre trade was in trouble, and prove they were essential. When the calendar returned in the Eighties, it was to a company and marketing department that kept exact track of what sold and what worked, and dealers who sold through what looked like ordinary shops, rather than racks at the corner of a greasy garage forecourt. Increasingly, the calendar seemed like good judgement. It was now a calculation, where once it had been a calculated risk. And while its profile in Milan was kept low until it was a success, it went on to be used internationally, a British product launched by Pirelli's subsidiaries around the world.

Things were very different at the start, in 1963. Pirelli was trying to sell tyres on their design, their newness, as well as their price; but it was hard for a UK company to have style. Style belonged to Chelsea, to Liverpudlians, to people who, while they made money, made it outside big corporations; both the Beatles' music and Mary Quant's frocks were no more than generalizations of art school life (mini-skirts, frosted faces, listening at night to R&B). All this was happening in a fractured, changeable London so that the new 'youth culture' (a very Sixties phrase) went further than, say, the flappers of the Twenties. It put Britain on a collision course with style.

Older people didn't like it, much. Only a few years back, London was bowlers and pinstripes and deference and pudding basin haircuts; debutante models stood in tweed, and thoughtful weeklies had only just begun to chart the fall of an empire after the Suez fiasco. People's memories did not encourage them to want much more than peace and comfort: they remembered war, Depression, Blitz and austerity, in that order. They were not all happy when Harold Macmillan came close to saying they had never had it so good; they worried about the end of National Service, self-denial. The nation's moral fibre seemed at risk from tailored suits, washing machines, continental holidays.

Worse still, the marketing men of the Fifties had found and christened a whole new phenomenon: the teenager. This creature lived in a gap which had newly opened, between childhood and work. Teenagers had money in their pockets, music of their own, a degree of independence, and enormous hope. Parents were reluctant to deprive their children, now there was choice and at least the start of plenty. But teenagers wrote their own rules and that fearlessness alarmed older people who valued propriety because, within living memory, it was all they had.

Now there was change you had to think about, not just change enforced by failing banks or falling bombs. You knew how tough things could be, but the children did not. To the teenager, older people talked of a life so sad and drab it was scarcely worth listening; everything could and should be remade, in the image of the teen. Anarchic new dances, the Madison, the Frug, invaded debutante balls.

The Beatles' fans trapped the Prime Minister in Heathrow, uncaringly, in their passion to see the Fab Four. Later, an archbishop and the Editor of *The Times* would attend an audience of Mick Jagger, freshly convicted of drug offences, to hear first hand the gospel of the young. Most visibly, when styles changed, they changed on the streets.

Park the Vespa, sidle down to Tiles, or any other of the basements around Leicester Square where the 'mods' assemble at lunch-time or night-time; girl or boy, the mod spends half a ten pound pay packet on looks: on minis and thigh-high skirts, kohl-black eyes and straight bangs for the girls, and that vital half-inch of starched white Brixton cuff for the boys. Cross the river at Chelsea Bridge, then as now, and find the rockers at the tea stand, a thin-ribbed tribe of defiant ones. Observe the 'tickets', dreaming of dancing on *Ready, Steady Go!*; they're always a vital few months behind the mods, the ones who got caught with 'purple

hearts' from pushers when they could simply have bought them from the chemists. Out of sight, in a basement, are the 'beats', who suffer from angst and doubts about existence; and the 'pseuds', who would love to be beats, except that it means leaving home.

These tribes all have uniforms that set them apart from (say) sports jacket, grey flannels, black shoes; their identity rests on style. They've even grown that style at home; the sweet sounds of Motown are giving way to Liverpool (Elvis has been in the army and doesn't count); the gear comes from Carnaby Street, made and changed fast. But although the look has changed, and is all important, it can be deceptive. Pseuds care about careers, tickets are just dreamers, and mods would never think of sleeping with their boyfriends; even beats ask each other, rather shiftily, if they've *done it yet*. The revolution, even the Rolling Stones, is still a way off.

Style has its first heroes. People know the name of Alec Issigonis because he designed the Mini; his design is about economy, suspension, and transverse mounted engines instead of cosmetic fins and grilles like tiaras mounted on a duchess. John Fitzgerald Kennedy is still President of the USA, which means style isn't just ruffles, frocks and decor any more. The Sunday paper has a colour magazine that's dedicated to a new elite – to photographers, models and designers.

They are people with the wrong jobs, and the wrong vowels, but they are social, commercial stars ('camp Cockney' will soon be *de rigueur* even for earls). Their annual income would pay three and a half Prime Ministers, send seventy sons to Eton or buy nine average London houses. They can be ace reporters, style gurus, salesmen and artists all at once. And the models, who were once either debs or tarts or able to do a passable imitation of one or the other, are now various and individual. Twiggy is tiny and Cockney; Jean Shrimpton has two dogs, eleven finches and an alliance with David Bailey. 'My nose turns up,' she says, 'my legs are long and make me look gawky. But my face is in.'

Pictures of women on a calendar are not a sideshow. They are about models and photographers, the new gossip-column stars; they are about being certified young, and therefore free of old-style doubt and pessimism and over-seriousness; they have style and they play with pleasures. The very point of the pictures is desire. 'Sexual intercourse,' Philip Larkin wrote, 'began in 1963 (which was rather late for me) – between the end of the Chatterley ban and the Beatles' first L.P.' Sex was the battle which made a whole generation think it must, after all, be involved in a revolution.

For 1963 was another country, and not just because of the thirty-shilling bottle of Bollinger, the five-pound TV licence, the Mini for £447 12s 6d. Librarians refused to let children, on an errand for their parents, collect the works of Ian Fleming in case they opened them on the way home. Dead and poetic writers were allowed a degree of sexual frankness since Lady Chatterley was tried and then published; live ones were still prosecuted and so was poor *Fanny Hill* in paperback (dead, but not serious enough). When Rudi Geinreich announced the topless dress, fashion editors did not dare print the pictures, and magistrates confirmed that the nipple was illegal. The Queen's housekeeper censored the stage, making sure that nudes stood still, that Hedda Gabler's pious servant did not cry out 'Jesus!'; he distinguished himself by finding the sermons of Martin Luther too strong for theatre audiences.

On screen, rough British movies dealt in expedient sex, unwanted pregnancy and love in grey Northern towns; but the Chief Constable of Manchester sent his men to inspect every film that did not have a 'U' certificate (each year they sat through *Snow White* again, since it was rated 'A'). Sex was the ever-interesting subject, endlessly and rather nervously discussed in the glossy magazines, not yet taken for granted. (Brigid Brophy declared man monogamous, woman polygamous on the grounds of how easily each was sexually satisfied.) Campaigns to change the law on some sexual behaviours were gaining support, just because the old guard did not believe such things could be talked about. Sexual wit was possible, but already women sometimes found it offensive, and said so; they objected, particularly, to a stocking ad which showed a woman with ball and chain ('won't run . . . will captivate').

There was a rush of faintly lascivious novels by pretty girls of twenty (Charlotte Bingham, Virginia Ironside); but they were all

*Pictures of women on a calendar have style, and they play with pleasures. 1963 was another country. Sex was the ever-interesting topic.*

about innocents who fended off 'sex maniacs' and 'leches'. 'My family,' said Bingham, 'don't tend towards sex really. I don't think I do, either.' In the middle of this confusion, the English discovered suddenly that they were not at all superior to sex; the result was black farce.

The Minister of Defence shared a girl with a Russian Naval attaché, and, in the embarrassment, it was somehow the girls and their friends who saw the inside of jails. One of his Cabinet colleagues called medical evidence to prove *he* was not the headless torso in the Polaroid in a Duke's divorce case; another was denying that taking tea with a clerk was evidence of homosexuality; yet another was not, it seemed, the dinner party guest who served the potatoes in nothing but a leather mask. Rumour and scandal confirmed everyone's prejudices – either that sex was trouble and disaster, or else that it was absurd and hypocritical to think that way.

Style, it sometimes seemed, was an anchor; the most trivial thing had become the most solid. A President was murdered, a Pope died; the men who stole £2.5 million from a mail train became heroes, and their loot the basis of a national treasure hunt: even Government reports that year were heady with talk of cities on stilts, universities for all. Thigh-length boots made women stride out on the streets with a proud independence impossible in high heels (a change of style which changed attitudes), and the contraceptive pill was expected to start a sexual revolution (because, oddly, it was the one method of contraception thought not to embarrass men).

Now a calendar is only a bright, promotional idea, and the Pirelli pictures are meant to tease as well as dazzle. But these pages hold up a mirror to our desires – what we wanted, what we could accept.

We see a celebration of lovely women, and how
men dream of them. We also see ourselves.

# 2

## AMONG FRIENDS

*. . . the calendar was warmth,*
*escape, holiday –*
*places you knew,*
*girls you'd like to know,*
*and a sense of summer ease . . .*

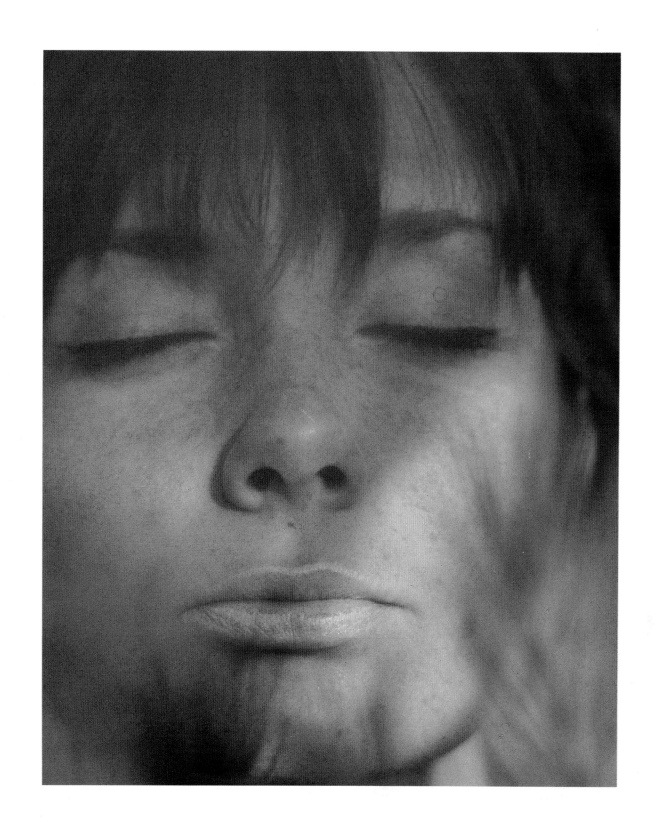

There was an air of informality about those early years – some girls, a trunk of clothes, a villa and a beach. Friends went abroad to make pictures together without fixed ideas, without a particular story to tell or filters and props to impose a particular kind of drama. It was enough to go to a pleasant place – to Majorca, where the tourist planes already landed in their dozens; to Monaco, and then, after the monstrous bills for lobster in the South of France, to the most sophisticated kind of package holiday in a Moroccan Club Med. (The English at the time went to Club Med in Corfu, and bragged about it; in Morocco there were only the French, chic by jowl.) You opened the calendar and, with luck, you might have been there; but perhaps not in such spectacular company.

Photographers who made fashion pictures were still allowed to be photo reporters; the calendar used the techniques of both. Naturalness was everything, a reaction to the spiky artifice of 1950s studio shots, but it was not naïvely natural. These pictures could pick out a detail for its graphic effect but, unlike the work of Bill Brandt who can make naked bodies into a landscape, the detail still had to be recognizably, enticingly, a woman. Behind the casual, effortless look was clever calculation.

They were confident pictures for times that seemed wonderfully sure: the Profumo affair had run its farcical course; Harold Wilson was talking of the 'white heat of the technological revolution'; and war was only a rumour – in Cyprus, Malaysia and the Gulf of Tonkin off Vietnam. But by the time the 1965 calendar was being made, those rumours had turned into shooting wars. Mods and rockers staged their own seaside battles, watched by airborne police and panicky reporters. The Beatles had become merchandise (berets, bedspreads, even Beatles pictures in a sixpenny pack of chewing gum) and rebellion belonged to the Rolling Stones – less couth, more middle class, more obviously renegades ('the time they use after shave,' said their co-manager Andrew Oldham, 'is the time they'll slip.').

The mini-skirt was in couture, thanks to Courrèges, and so was the peasant dress at Saint Laurent; natural wholefood reached the King's Road ('brawn from the natural pig . . .'); comprehensive schools had started; the eye was battered by the stripy conundrums of op art, and a protester walked off with Goya's portrait of the Duke of Wellington, only to abandon it in Lost Property at Birmingham Station. The landmarks of swinging London were opening up – Alvaro's and the discotheque Sybilla's in 1966; Robert Fraser's gallery and boutiques like Granny Takes a Trip were already there. The energy and flash were formidable, and they had not yet calcified into institutions. 'Management,' says Derek Forsyth, 'asked me what the plans for 1964 advertising were, and I didn't have a clue. There was money to give things away, and my boss was on holiday in Mozambique, so I said we were going to produce a calendar. It wouldn't be a grand production – just £2,000 to take some models to Majorca for a week.'

He took with him the stars of the Sixties – models, photographers, designers. As friends, they all unwittingly launched a phenomenon.

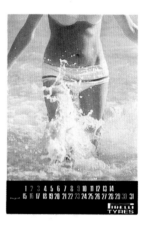

# 1964: Robert Freeman in Majorca

The ads were avant-garde at the time – they sold tyres without showing cars – and the photographer was a talented newcomer called Robert Freeman. (It was a time when almost all successful photographers were newcomers; no stigma was attached.) He had been a professional for only two years, but he had captured mods and rockers for the *Sunday Times* colour magazine, and movie and travel stories and a memorable image of the tail fin of a Cadillac parked before Big Ben for a story on the English taste for Americana; he had shot fashion for *Queen* magazine and he was very soon to fix the grainy, early image of the Beatles on their first album covers. But more important, he had made for *Town* magazine some discreetly but distinctly sexy pictures of his wife, Sonny.

Sexy had not yet come to mean anatomical, remember; erotic did not demand a full inventory of body parts, all visibly accounted for. Sexy could be decorative, and a window into what a woman wanted; her look mattered as much as the man's right to look at her. Such pictures could even grow out of a marriage, because there was nothing casual about them. You did not go out to groom some smooth, perfect woman chosen from a catalogue; you might plan the pictures, as Freeman did, while his wife was heavily pregnant with their second child. Three weeks after Sonny gave birth, she was on the plane to Majorca.

She was to be the redhead, Jane Lumb the blonde; the casting was that simple. To Jane Lumb, it seemed wonderfully casual and friendly. She had just flunked her Oxford entrance exams, and she

was waiting to hear from London University; a friend had suggested she might as well try modelling, something to fill in time and fund what was still a student round of pubs and tandoori. She had learned already the upside down snobbery of her new world – the accent grew more raw, her uncle the Colonel had to be forgotten; she was ready to be one of the true Sixties figures, when finally they emerged. To Derek Forsyth she seemed the perfect girl next door.

After a few failed auditions, the calendar was her first proper, paid job. 'There was no really big deal about it at the time,' she says, 'we were just off to Majorca for a week to make some nice pictures. But I did think that if every job was going to be like this, modelling would suit me very well.'

The team set up house in a rented farmhouse, down by the beach – Derek Forsyth, Sonny and Robert Freeman, and Jane Lumb. Jane was the wild card. It seemed logical she should be photographed first while Sonny rested, got into condition, and began to brown. But during the daytime, Sonny was alone and trying to rest, surrounded by gabbling chickens, a new baby and an especially large cleaning woman, who could bustle at the top of her voice. She found it hard to accept the ordinary, professional fact that her husband was down on the beach with another model, working at the kind of pictures Sonny should be in. She had worked only with Robert, and Robert usually worked with her. It seemed like an invasion.

*Down by the beach, Jane was the wild card . . . The calendar was meant to be playful it was the early phase of those freewheeling attitudes.*

'I was incredibly jealous, anyway,' Sonny says; Robert Freeman remembers, more discreetly, 'some territorial feeling.' But one night, Sonny's anger spilled over, and she let Robert know her feelings in no uncertain terms.

Her fretfulness had vanished by the time she went before the camera. She stands, her hand straying under a borrowed shirt, looking at her man rather than into the impersonal lens; 'a look,' she says, 'of sweet, tempting love, if you like. If you work with

someone you know well, it shows.' It was intimate, but it was almost modest because it is so obviously loving, the exact opposite of the brazen glamour shot; you look, and you are involved. In the very close shot of Sonny's face, Robert Freeman says, 'there could be things going on either in her mind or outside the frame'; but you have to imagine them. It is a frame from a drama; even the idea of such a tight close-up is 'big screen influence'.

'It was,' he says, 'like doing my own pictures with Sonny – images that I liked. If you like girls, then they're flowers in the garden – there are different moods and moments, and it's nice to capture them. And I've always loved the very early Goya paintings – that warm, fluffy, light-headed, airy feel, like being in love with the subject.

'We thought of a graphic approach, close-ups, parts of bodies, simple and intimate; Derek wanted the paper to be matt to get away from the glossy calendar associations. It was meant to be

playful and easy in its attitudes. Remember, it was the early phase of those freewheeling attitudes – I'd say permissive, but that's a bit of a pompous word.'

There was none of the now essential helpers – no stylist to realize the photographer's ideas, no hair-dresser or make-up artist; the props were a few simple beach clothes. 'I was able to get on with the work,' Freeman says, 'without a big team staring – when you have all of them, it shows in the picture because I respond differently and the model responds differently.' Each location was talked about, analysed, but it might be something as simple as a deckchair on the beach and the pattern it cast on a body, and then Freeman was left to work as though making his own experiments, or reporting a story for a magazine. He used only natural light, without even a reflector, and fast 35mm film; the warm shadows on the skin, the gentleness of the colour come from shooting close to sunrise and sunset.

Forsyth and his team brought back their calendar, assembled it, and saw it duly distributed to dealers. Perhaps better not send it to Milan. The English, learning to freewheel, felt uneasy about how their new venture would be received in an Italian boardroom.

There was no grand launch, no public relations effort, and no response from the newspapers. What did happen, though, was that Pirelli began to get letters from dealers; for some reason Pirelli, after the calendar, was suddenly popular.

Majorca, 1964. Robert Freeman
photographs Jane Lumb.
Calendar picture on right.

First-timer Jane Lumb – the perfect girl next door, as this calendar picture suggests. On right, Jane Lumb over twenty years later.

Jane Lumb

Left, Sonny Freeman photographed
by her husband, Robert Freeman.
Now Sonny Drane, here she is with
her family.

Sonny Drane/Freeman

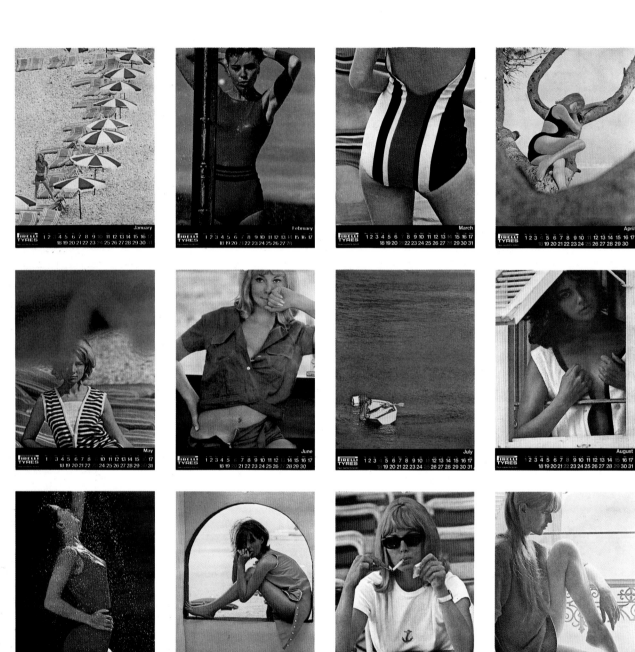
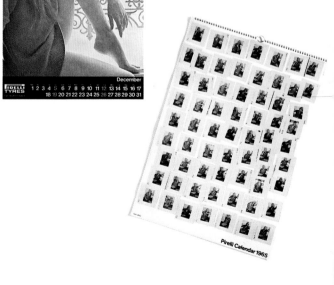

Pirelli Calendar 1965

# 1965: Brian Duffy in the South of France

'The way to do a calendar with a fairly high element of sex,' Colin Forbes says, 'was to put the girls in some natural setting like the beach. Putting girls on tractors was not the answer.'

The beach suggested holiday, an escape from the locker-room or office; it also made undressing natural. That had advantages beyond the obvious one of showing flesh. A woman on the beach can be anyone you want – the princess, a shopgirl, a model, with no social signs to spoil the range of fantasy; you can imagine meeting her, casually, and you're licensed to look. One woman is waving by the beach umbrellas, another is waiting within an arch by the beach, her fingers playing at her mouth; you are welcome, not an intruder.

Forbes was the designer and Derek Forsyth the producer; Pirelli

*In the social hierarchy of 1964 there were three East Enders who became stars: David Bailey, Terence Donovan and Brian Duffy. 'Most photographers are butterflies . . .'*

had fired its ad agency and was creating its own image. Brian Duffy was the photographer, known for his sharp look at women. They borrowed a fine Edwardian apartment in Monaco from an expatriate aunt of a friend, and struggled to find it from a description – not even an address. They found it, and for ten days went looking for pictures.

The process was a collaboration, at least until the moment Duffy raised the camera; then, everything hung on the precision with which he saw the subject, how he edited expressions and gestures. An art director sees shapes and stories, but only the photographer puts life into the design. Look again at the girl in a red swimsuit under a beach shower; you can see the water is cold, and that she is pleasurably stung by it. The image of Pauline Stone, tangled in the branches of a gnarled and silvery tree, came from Duffy's roadside discovery of the prop, and his quick suggestion of how to use it. 'It helps,' Pauline Stone says, 'that Duffy made women look beautiful. He was actually nice to women.'

In the social hierarchy of 1964, there were three East Enders who had become stars: David Bailey, Terence Donovan, and Brian Duffy. They were the 'photogenes', living by the art of the camera – social cavaliers with suspect accents but the correct Sixties career. Photographers were becoming so dazzling that they rather obscured the designers who planned, cropped and presented their work.

Duffy had been making pictures for the Cinturato tyre, shots in a cobbled Belgian backstreet in the wet; he was next in line for the calendar. He had the reputation of an ideas man and a technical wizard. After art school, he had set out to design frocks and sell antiques – those were occupations proper for a family man in the Sixties – but he was sidetracked by an apprenticeship at *Vogue*. He carried with him socialist convictions ('which I think he used to wind people up,' Pauline Stone says), a taste for abstract nouns and long discussion, and a generosity which kept his studio gently irrigated with champagne.

His job could sometimes be obscured by the column inches. When Bailey married Catherine Deneuve, Duffy signed the register alongside Mick Jagger. With Len Deighton, Duffy later worked on the movie version of *Oh! What A Lovely War,* that bitter vaudeville about the First World War. The cast of a dinner at Alvaro's would be Michael Caine, Terence Stamp, maybe a mogul like Harry Saltzman and Brian Duffy. There were even long articles on Brian Duffy's theories of child rearing, not an occupation much connected with the King's Road.

'Most photographers,' he said at the time, 'are butterflies. We work from flair, that debatable area where you're not sure whether it's absolutely the most awful taste you've ever seen, or it's really the most marvellous good taste.' In those words he betrayed an early boredom with still images.

But his eye and timing were very precise. Look again at the girl in a café, lighting a cigarette, a cliché of French or maybe even Casablanca life. What makes the picture work is the way the girl's breasts so nearly, closely brush the table, but not quite. The tension is the picture, and it is Duffy's particular contribution.

He drove, of course, a Sprite; he set out for Monaco with (of course) a model, Pauline Stone. There were to be six models, arriving three at a time, and all staying in that grand apartment with Duffy, Forbes and Forsyth. The last two had shared some lively bachelor days, and Colin Forbes' wife Wendy was suspicious.

She was convinced of wickedness to come. Six months pregnant, she gave Forbes an ultimatum as he set out for France; she had her

ticket home to Australia, and she was packed. Forbes persuaded her to cancel that trip and come, instead, on the shoot. She saw the models as he saw them – 'horrendous, slightly bitchy girls who all argued', Forbes remembers; they seemed more like aggravation than temptation. Instead of breaking a marriage, those ten days cemented it.

The men, at least, worked in remarkable harmony. Derek Forsyth was not yet designing the calendar but producing it. 'He was the Diaghilev if you like,' says Forbes. 'One of our problems is that we don't have enough Diaghilevs, even though there are lots of talented people; the key to doing something wonderful is the producer.' Forsyth impressed Duffy one evening by sitting down to sketch the eight images they had already made. 'He managed to draw what I had in the viewfinder,' Duffy said, with wonder.

The three collaborated on the trademark of the early Pirelli calendars: the too-close shot of a detail of a body, a graphic idea which belongs in some measure to the art director. It is his job to watch the details – the corner of a shutter, the wrought iron of a balcony – which will eventually imply to the audience somewhere warm, Mediterranean and desirable.

Derek Forsyth, meanwhile, had a different problem. The budget for the calendar was still sensible rather than generous, and the restaurants of the South of France are never cheap; the girls seemed to have an insatiable appetite for lobster, or whatever else was most expensive on the menu. The meals cost as much as the rest of the trip put together, which accounts for the times that later calendars were made in places served by package holidays.

It was still only a gift for the trade, very far from its later status. But while Duffy's images were hanging on the garage walls, one significant thing changed. Milan had been wondering; but soon was to be astonished. Pirelli UK hired a new public relations man, a journalist called Robert Newman, and he had the bright idea of launching the calendar to the Press and public, not just the trade. He began to consider the ways and means to hype these friendly pictures into a reputation for Pirelli.

Monaco 1965. Jeannette Harding on the beach. This was the photograph originally chosen for the calendar, with her hand at her breast. But it was felt to be too suggestive, and another was chosen. The strip is from the same shoot.

At the beach bar. This picture of
Jeannette Harding got as far as proof
stage and was shown to Pirelli along
with the other twelve pictures.
Predictably, it was discarded as
too wild.

Four frames from the same shoot as the
wild one above.

Annabella and Virginia perhaps
growing impatient with the length of
time this photograph took in the
setting-up, play provocatively.
Not used.

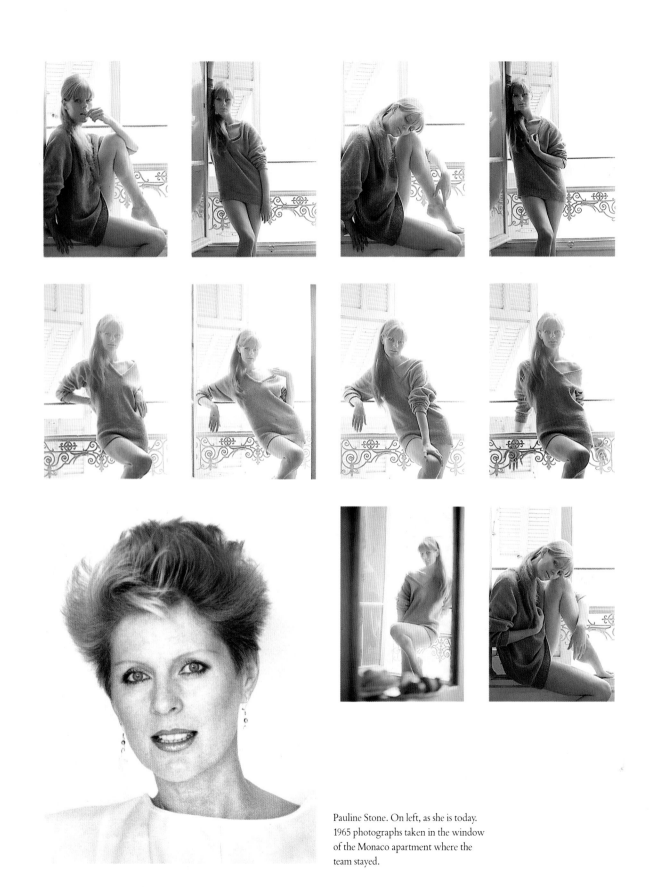

Pauline Stone. On left, as she is today.
1965 photographs taken in the window
of the Monaco apartment where the
team stayed.

Pauline Dukes. These photographs were designed deliberately to evoke the holiday snap. Those who saw the calendar felt they might do as well.

Annabella

Pauline Stone

Annabella

# 1966: Peter Knapp in Morocco

Peter Knapp was a part-time Londoner – trained in Zurich, based in Paris but close to the life of the King's Road; it was Brian Duffy who told him about the Pirelli Calendar. 'You have to remember that in the Sixties it was the beginning of taking a plane and going to another town,' Knapp says. 'Before that, it was very exotic to go all the way to London or to Paris. All of a sudden, you could do it each week.'

Knapp was sceptical about the calendar at first. 'I'm not so keen on making sexy pictures. I often think people are very interested by the girl and not so interested by how the picture is done.

'But it was an interest to see nude women – especially to see the good women nude. You had always the 'model', what the French call *photos de charme* and the porno stuff, but in the 1960s it was fashionable to be tanned all over. So girls were prepared to be nude. It was the start of *féminisme*.'

At *Elle*, the French fashion magazine, he had stopped the chic, affected poses of the Fifties; he made pictures that were more realistic, and more sensual because the blood was back in the bodies he photographed. His calendar is sometimes much the same as a fashion assignment – see the girls together in their blue bikinis – and not only because the models are often dressed. One or two of the faces did later appear in *Elle*; the girl in the black wetsuit, at the time an air hostess, is one of them.

'What we did in the calendar,' Knapp says, 'was already the limit

of what you could do then.' The models were careful, the client scrupulous, unlike today: 'You want to do topless, they call it lingerie and it's double the price.'

At that time, sexy meant only *Playboy*, and the choice of models for the calendar meant it was bound to be different. For Knapp the auditions, held in London, were the usual ordeal. 'The girl finds herself in a bad situation,' he

*'In the 1960s girls were prepared to be nude. What we did in the calendar was already the limit of what you could do then.'*

says, 'because it's raining, and she arrives with a raincoat and we are in this room and we tell her to put on a bathing suit. She does not feel like it. Then, when she has it on, she has a very white body, and she finds herself ugly; the psychology is all wrong for us to decide if we will take her or not.' He is grateful that colour Polaroids and, above all, video have made the process less arbitrary.

Derek Forsyth's and Colin Forbe's theme was simple: 'Fashion girls go for holidays to Club Méditerranée – girls on the beach, on bikes, on horses.' For the English, the Club was still unfamiliar, and even for the French, the straw-hut villages in North Africa were something new. But the atmosphere of holiday almost disrupted Knapp's usual precise ways of working.

Precision was, after all, why Peter Knapp became a photographer in the first place. As an art director of magazines, he was often frustrated by the problems of getting some simple, but exact picture that he needed. Good photographers would refuse such a confining job, and bad ones would botch it. 'It was easier to do it myself,' Knapp says.

He directs exactly, even showing models sketches of what he wants;

the graphic idea is always clear from the start – 'which doesn't mean that, in the end, the picture is the way I saw it. Often it doesn't work at all.' The functions of photographer and art director come very close together.

But this time, the most he had was an occasional storyboard for long shots – horses riding along the beach, for example – 'a little like an amateur movie. I'm absolutely not a reporter photographer, but this time the pictures were not made. They were taken. And often I had the girls doing things together while I was making pictures of only one – I created holiday scenes and they rarely knew when I was shooting.'

Worse, Knapp was having a rough passage with Rita, his own girlfriend, a very successful model who never seemed to fit the model mould. Rita had refused to be in the calendar at all, because she did not like to be paid to look sexy. At first, Knapp was a little relieved; the other models could have no suspicion that he was favouring his lover. But once he was in Morocco, the reality was more bleak – Rita was in New York, and Club Med had everything except telephones.

He was patient with the girls, even when it turned out that not one of them could ride a horse, as all of them had promised; a gallop through the waves had to become a polite stroll along the beach, and that took two and a half days to achieve. Knapp's telephoto picture had the grave disadvantage that the girls, three hundred yards away, could not hear his instructions, and their private semaphore turned out to be ambiguous.

For once, he could not simply rely on his assistant – the porter, gofer, dogsbody of the trade. Bloch-Lainé struggled with the huge reflectors that Knapp used, and his own hopeless calf-love for a Eurasian model; the producers still remember his desolate face pressed against an airport fence as she left. Love was some consolation for an assistant's

*A girl stands in a straw hut, lit red by the sunset, looking in a mirror; her body is bare, but cossetted by her underwear . . .*

life, always subordinate to what the master wants; 'really,' Knapp says, 'a slave. But he is paying the price to be with a master he likes, and all of my assistants have gone on to be photographers.' Bloch-Lainé is now one of the finest still-life photographers in Paris; he remembers the days in Morocco. 'I didn't fall in love,' he says. 'At least, I didn't fall in love any more than I always do.' He sighs.

One time only, Knapp was asked to do a picture that was deliberately 'sexy'. A girl stands in a straw hut, lit red by the sunset, looking in a mirror; her body is bare, but cossetted by the straps and translucency of her underwear; it's so casual that you seem to share the hut and you could almost move forward to hold her. It could easily have turned into a fetish snap – Knapp happened to find the new transparent lingerie very sexy; the calendar's audience fancied it could see more than was there, and there was great controversy. But the result is lovely, and almost domestic. You're invited to share the holiday, not just to gawp.

For the first time, the calendar that year was not just for the dealers; it was launched to the Press. Robert Newman hired the

Carlton Tower Hotel, engineered a special Moroccan menu, and sent out eighty-five invitations.

On the day, Newman stood anxiously at the door, certain he would be fired; he could count only twelve reporters in the huge room. The event was extravagant and, worse still, it was unusual; if it went wrong, nobody would rush to share the blame. He had meant to keep the calendar exclusive – 4,000 were for the public at large, out of a print order of 28,000 – but it looked as though he might unwittingly have killed it through understatement.

He scanned the papers anxiously next morning. There was only one story – in the diary of the newly launched, serious-minded, worthy *Sun* – but that was enough. Pirelli, like all other makers of unromantic car parts, was used to battling for space even in specialized magazines; but here was a friendly, lengthy mention in a national paper. The managers, in their panelled offices, were delighted.

Milan's reaction was more stern. There seems to have been a sense, helped by private talk, that the calendar was not proper for a good Italian family concern; the rumour was Vatican intervention, which, in the rather strait-laced Italy of the time, did not need to be direct or formal. There were other factors nearer home. The

Cinturato tyre, the all-textile radial, was now an outstanding success; but there had been credit squeezes as a nervous Chancellor of the Exchequer tried to stave off the devaluation of the pound. So why did Pirelli need to talk to a public that had no money to spend, especially with the barely clothed bottom of a model?

At the time, the calendar was easy to kill.

Morocco, 1966. Television cameras capture a moment in the making of the Pirelli calendar. Colin Forbes, Peter Knapp and Derek Forsyth look on.

The first experiment of featuring
a man in the calendar turned
out to be the last. It was
felt that the male presence
destroyed the illusion which the
calendar created – the dream of
a girl alone and maybe accessible.

A blithely innocent subject is
being filmed above, but the
angle had yet to be plotted by
the art director and the
eventual picture cropped –
on right.

Shirley Ann today. The
Knapp/Pirelli assignment was one
of her first modelling jobs, and she
found it – despite her initial fears –
both relaxed and professional. As
she looks back, the job is still the
highlight of her ten years' career as
a model. She is now a property
developer, and lives in London
with her three children.

# 3

## LOVE AND GLAMOUR

*. . . after the easy years came*
*flower power, surfer chic*
*and a careful beauty*
*that improved on nature;*
*love was a slogan, war was real . . .*

The easy years were soon gone, with their sunshine confidence and their playfulness. By the end of the Sixties the agenda was love and glamour, and everyone wanted a meaning. They might find it in revolution, with an Eastern guru, in sex or on a sugarcube or in a puff of weed; but it had to be sought and worked at.

The Beatles had Maharishi Mahesh Yoga, and the Apple Shop where flower children milled and bought (and shoplifted, the downfall of the business); members of the Rolling Stones, according to the police courts, chose the chemical road to expanded consciousness. You could be right – mystical or revolutionary, or even both at once – 'Make Love Not War' was an order.

The openness, the surf and music from America was enticing; but that sunny dream was to be broken up by protests at the war in Vietnam, the killing of Martin Luther King and Robert Kennedy and the racial conflicts on city streets. London played at the same civil war, but cops and radicals sang 'Auld Lang Syne' at midnight. Paris played harder, with cobblestones and tear gas; but after the revolution, Navy blazers were suddenly as obligatory on the Left Bank as the image of Che Guevara (killed in 1967) once had been.

In Britain the tribal wars of mods and rockers had long gone, replaced by hippies (soft, long-haired, gentle creatures who loved relentlessly) and skinheads (vicious, envious, uninquisitive kids who distilled their anger like a cordial). Sex was politics, and a human right – 'the Pursuit of the Holy Wail', *Esquire* said. The micro-mini appeared, but so too did faded, flowing dresses that seemed to stem from some soft Pre-Raphaelite dream; the female eunuch, newly christened by Germaine Greer, looked feminine.

Class came back, suddenly. Movies were interested again in the upper classes, ambition and glamour; the Kray twins, gangster East Enders once considered chic, were jailed, but they were also out of date. The designer cult reached national ceremonies; everyone knew that Snowdon designed the Investiture of the Prince of Wales. The youth cult had its first crisis; Pat Booth was twenty-five when she appeared in the 1968 calendar, and ready to retire. 'When you hit twenty-five you might as well die; we all thought that.'

The dealers demanded the calendar's return; the reps were lost on the road without it. But it would be a very different style for the late Sixties. The *Sunday Times* complained: 'The bedroom door has been taken off its hinges, thighs have been exposed in the streets and genitals on the screen and in the theatre.' That was even before the first topless model at the Motor Show (1969); the first on Page Three of the *Sun* newspaper (1970); and the stunning announcement that Mary Quant had trimmed her pubic hair in the shape of a heart.

Glamour was almost obligatory.

January Gennaio Januar Janvier

February Febbraio Februar Février

March Marzo März Mars

April Aprile April Avril

May Maggio Mai Mai

June Giugno Juni Juin

July Luglio Juli Juillet

August Agosto August Août

September Settembre September Septembre

October Ottobre Oktober Octobre

November Novembre November Novembre

December Dicembre Dezember Decembre

January Gennaio Januar Janvier

# 1968: Harri Peccinotti in Tunisia

It was the year after 'All You Need Is Love', when feeling was everything; the year of cults and gurus and mystical faith, when even the Monkees, creatures of the commercial break, chanted 'I'm a Believer' (but only in love); and the year of chemicals supposed to bend, expand and kaleidoscope the consciousness. Indulgence was a virtue, reticence a sin. Naturally, people wrote about it.

It is an open question whether many read the poems, but they were piled high in basement bookstores, chanted at public meetings, discussed and analysed; the words to any Beatles song were classified poems, so that everyone had something to discuss.

The calendar team found poems about love – some Japanese, some Elizabethan, some ancient and some from Allen Ginsberg and Elizabeth Barrett Browning; they found girls to match the words, and they planned pictures that were to be much more than simple illustrations. For this, Forsyth and his team went away to the island of Djerba, off Tunisia – in legend, the home of the lotus eaters – and they settled, for economy's sake, in a brand-new Club Med.

The photographer was Harri Peccinotti who, like Peter Knapp, was an art director whose impatience had turned him into a photographer. The models, like the poems, were from across the world, which was still unusual. Peccinotti had used black models in pictures for *Nova* in 1963, but that was considered daring and even a touch gimmicky; now he had a black model, a Chinese woman, almost as much of a rarity in print, and a Scandinavian so pale she

seemed translucent. Ulla Randall is that white, white lady stretched out in the pale morning sun, the picture subtly underexposed and shot against the faint light ('More white than whitest Lillies far . . .').

There was also Pat Booth, nursing an eye infection, and resigned to the fact that somehow Harri Peccinotti always photographed parts of her body, never the whole. ('I was,' she says, 'bigger than most girls.') There was a French model who yearned, and pleaded, to go back to her rock star boyfriend, and did indeed leave early; and one whose boyfriend contrived to arrive, on the remote island of Djerba, in a shiny black stretch limo. He wore his Italian accent and his black and white brogues like a threat.

'We were a little like football hooligans,' Peccinotti says, 'with models.' They were in an Islamic country where women covered themselves; but somehow, each time a model undressed for the camera, a posse of Arabs would appear on the dunes, looking fierce and disapproving; however far away the team went, the Arabs were already there. 'We were always trying not to upset people,' he says, 'but models are quite good at flaunting themselves in places where they're least expected to, and wondering why they get into trouble.'

Some pictures were planned from the very start – Peccinotti had brought a shirt from Soho Sportique whose red, blue and white exactly matched the stripes around an air mail envelope ('I marvelled, my beloved, when I read thy thought so in the letter . . .') and a sunflower to go with an Allen Ginsberg poem ('We're all beautiful golden sunflowers . . .'). Where a poem mentioned a wet skirt, or waiting on a beach, the cues were obvious; but the bare shoulder ('this morning I will not comb my hair . . .'), the voluminous dark woman moving, double-exposed, before a

Mahgreb house ('when as in silks my Julia goes . . .'), and the particular, close look of Jill la Tour under her braided hair ('whatever else you do, please don't look at me that way . . .') are inspirations.

The poems were less euphemistic than the pictures had to be. A woman lies on a beach, about to wake; she must be naked, but propriety has clipped away the nipple from the picture. 'The only place you saw nipples,' Peccinotti says, 'was in dirty bookshops, for a market of underground sex.' A long shirt blows wetly against a woman's body, but there is no shadow of hair; the fact that it was touched out makes its absence quite shocking now.

> *It was radical to put love and words on the garage wall, a risk . . . it was not what the trade expected.*

But it was radical to put love and words on the garage wall, a risk despite the glowing response of the Press; it was not what the trade expected, and it might seem to be aimed over their heads. There was little time to worry while the wine was copious, and the alliances conveniently changing so as not to spoil the shoot. There seemed to be all the time in the world . . . when the calendar was nearly lost.

Half way through the shoot, Djerba was buzzed by low-flying aircraft. On the one portable radio in the Club Med, the team could vaguely make out English-language reports from Libya telling Americans to move out, and with only one suitcase; they could not tell if the trouble was local, or global.

They were in an Islamic country with pictures of women, which was trouble enough, but also they had a Mini-Moke which counted as a desert vehicle, a trunk full of the cartridge belts which were then thought chic (some of the unused poems were about the Mexican revolution) and no explanation that any frontier policeman would be inclined to believe, even without a war.

Harri Peccinotti went out first. The keys to the Mini-Moke had to be found; he spent a morning digging like a dog in the river of sand that ran beneath the wattle huts. He took the ferry to the mainland, and then, as dark was falling, set off on a short cut across the desert.

The sand slowed him down, and the dogs ran up from Tuareg tents along the road, and Peccinotti was beating them off with a water bottle; in his imagination, they were lions.

He reached Tunis to find the main square full of tanks – Moroccan tanks, passing through to the front. For the first time, he discovered exactly what was happening: Israel and the Arab states were at war. He was interested, as any veteran of reporting Vietnam would be. That night, he went out dressed in a *djellaba* to photograph the burning of the British Embassy; a Moroccan policeman tackled him, put him under house arrest in his hotel and took away all his film except, oddly, for what was in the camera. Derek Forsyth, too, was stopped at the coast and questioned. The Pirelli Calendar now needed a hero.

Rodney Kinsman was then, he says, 'an embryonic furniture designer and occasional model'; he had come to Tunisia with his wife, the model Elisa Ngai – 'not as a chaperone,' he says, 'not entirely . . .' He was less than welcome at first, but he proved to be the only horseman in the team who could keep up with the rough-riding Arabs, and the best builder of defences against the sandstorms which turned the floors of the Club Med huts into quicksand. But, much more to the point, he had a ticket out directly from Djerba to London. When the trouble blew up, Forsyth had thought to entrust him with the bulk of the film. Kinsman left, a little after the main party, and took the film home without questions. The calendar was saved.

It made a fine story, at the launch.

Tunisia, 1968. Inspired by the poem, Elisa Ngai sits on the hot sands. Above, Elisa with her husband Rodney Kinsman. She is now a cookery writer while he designs furniture.

*You do not come, and I wait*
*On Matsuo beach,*
*In the calm of evening.*
*And like the blazing*
*Water, I too am burning.*

FUJIWARA NO SADAIE 1162–1242

Ulla Randall

*You are the bouquet of your own bouquet:*
*The fairest flower that's there mid grace and green*
*Since from your breath the fragrance caught its sheen;*
*For it, like me, is pale with love all day.*

*If then a flower may love you too, I say*
*(And all inept your virtue now to glean)*
*How should I feel who all your charms have seen,*
*Who grieve and serve in knowledge as I may?*

*E'en as a flower is withered in a day,*
*I fear your love will wither all too soon:*
*A woman's love is fickle as the moon.*

*Whatever destiny shall bring my way,*
*He cannot steal my memory of you—*
*Unless he tear my mind and heart out too.*

PIERRE DE RONSARD 1524–1585

Ulla Randall

Marie, arise, away with slothfulness!
Already to the skies the lark has sung,
The nightingale full sweetly has begun
Beneath the thorn his lovely plaintiveness!

Come, up! and see the grassy dewiness,
Your rose tree all with budding blossoms hung,
The darling pinks you watered one by one
With your own hand last night in gentleness!

Yestreen as you lay down you vowed to be
Up and awake ere I might stir today;
But dawn's own dreams which fair maids ever see.

Hold your eyes shut and wakefulness away.
See, see, a hundred times I kiss your eyes,
Your little breast: My love, 'tis morn! Arise!

PIERRE DE RONSARD 1524–1585

57

Elisa Ngai. These photographs were prompted by the poem by Yamabe No Akahito. The pubic hair was masked out for the printed calendar picture.

*I wish I were close*
*To you as the wet skirt of*
*A salt girl to her body*
*I think of you always.*

*YAMABE NO AKAHITO 8TH CENT.*

Elisa Ngai

*Is it indeed so? If I lay here dead,*
*Wouldst thou miss any life in losing mine?*
*And would the sun for thee more coldly shine*
*Because of grave-damps falling around my head?*
*I marvelled, my Beloved, when I read*
*Thy thought so in the letter. I am thine –*
*But . . . so much to thee? Can I pour thy wine*
*Whilst my hands tremble? Then my soul, instead*
*Of dreams of death, resumes life's lower range.*
*Then, love me, Love! Look on me – breathe on me!*
*As brighter ladies do not count it strange,*
*For love, to give up acres and degree,*
*I yield the grave for thy sake, and exchange*
*My near sweet view of heaven, for earth with thee!*

ELIZABETH BARRETT BROWNING 1806–1861

Pat Booth, now a best-selling novelist
living in California. Far right, Pat
Booth as the famous sunflower symbol
– later she was made to float on
solid black. Above right, variation on
the same theme.

*We're not our skin of grime, we're not our dread bleak*
*dusty imageless locomotive, we're all beautiful golden sunflowers*
*inside, we're blessed by our own seed & golden hairy naked*
*accomplishment – bodies growing into mad black formal sunflowers*
*in the sunset, spied on by our eyes under the shadow of the*
*mad locomotive riverbank sunset Frisco hilly tincan evening*
*sitdown vision.*

ALLEN GINSBERG 1926–

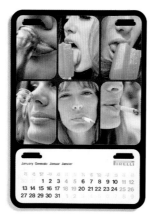

January Gennaio Januar Janvier

February Febbraio Februar Février

March Marzo März Mars

April Aprile April Avril

May Maggio Mai Mai

June Giugno Juni Juin

July Luglio Juli Juillet

August Agosto August Août

September Settembre September Septembre

October Ottobre Oktober Octobre

November Novembre November Novembre

December Dicembre Dezember Décembre

CALIFORNIA
PIR 1969

# 1969: Harri Peccinotti in California

1968 was the last summer of simple dreams about America – that half patronizing, half admiring European sense of America as the cousin who went abroad and did well. The reality of the war in Vietnam was becoming inescapable, the Tet offensive was a catastrophe; Lyndon Johnson was about to give up any hope of being re-elected, and the war went bloodily to the streets of Chicago.

Then again, there was California – definitely America, but a dream state more than a material State of the Union. It was golden bodies, surf and palms and sand, dune buggies and Gidget and Beach Boys music, the Hollywood stars and the Mamas and the Papas, a euphoric hunt for pleasure; it was seductive, and it might even be our future – freeways, cults, smog, hallucinogens and pizza-by-phone included. It was being young and on holiday as a way of life, just as the calendar demanded; it was our paradoxical sunrise in the West.

Harri Peccinotti had been thankfully stuck there, working on the titles for a movie which was delayed. He went out to Newport for the legendary jazz, a little startled that the Lighthouse club turned out to be less than grand, and he jammed and hung out with the groups who were turning Los Angeles into a rock capital. He was hot to go back, and he saw the calendar as his ticket. 'California,' he says, 'was really my fault.'

His idea was simply to report. 'Everywhere you turned on the beach there were incredible looking girls,' he remembers, 'just very sexy girls and they were taking their clothes off and doing whatever they felt like – it was a very free time. I said we wouldn't have to take models or anything; we'd just go and photograph people having a good time in the sun.'

Derek Forsyth and the group settled in luxury – a brief lease on a Bel Air mansion which once belonged to the late Tyrone Power, with a white piano and floors of fur, and a swimming pool in which a huge black preacher one afternoon surprised Peccinotti. 'He was looking for money and he addressed me as Mr Tyrone Power,' Peccinotti says. 'I told him if I was, I could tell him a few things he could use.'

But Peccinotti's California, all lovely women in the great white curls of the Pacific, was not there. 'There was no surf, and all the kids were on holiday somewhere else; they only go to the local beach on schooldays. We chased surf up and down that coast. We called the phone surf service and they sent us to Newport or Big Sur, and we'd find huge surf and not a soul in sight, or else a few muscly lads, which was not what we wanted; or a beach looking like Nice in August.'

The glow of surfing gold was quickly fading, under a gunmetal sky; but, in 1968, it was remarkable, and expensive, to go to California, and something had to be done. There were no model agencies in a city without a rag trade, and the would-be starlets, some attached to friends, were unused to the idea of still pictures that didn't lead to moving pictures.

*'Everywhere you turned on the beach there were incredible looking girls, sexy girls and they were taking their clothes off . . .'*

They posed around a swimming pool, tongues busy on ice popsicles, lips busy on Coca Cola bottles, concepts which were strong for the time. 'We thought of doing a whole calendar around the mouth.' But no company board could have approved it; besides, they would ask about the bill for pictures that could have been made in Streatham.

Peccinotti resorted to a topless bar on Sunset Strip called the Classic Cat, a drinking place with competent music whose star attraction was an amateur strip night ('amateur, I think, in the sense that the girls never got paid'). The compère introduced 'ordinary girls – she's a secretary from Pasadena and how about taking your clothes off, honey?' – and ended with an assortment of bodies on stage, waiting to see which one took the prize. Peccinotti sat at the back with a long lens, observing the oddly wholesome and undistracting jiggles under a reddish light ('it was very quiet with applause now and then, mostly when asked for').

But most of the calendar was snatched – on freeways, on the pier at

**'We thought of doing a whole calendar around the mouth . . . The girls on the beach signed nothing. The lawyer's advice was that we shouldn't be doing it . . .'**

Muscle Beach, at Newport by Peccinotti's own favourite jazz clubs. 'We were sitting around on the beach all day, with longish sort of lenses, and nobody was worrying too much. We asked if we could take pictures, or we took the pictures and asked later.'

Now a model's picture is useless, unless he or she has signed a release – a form which gives permission for the picture to be used. The girls on the beach, and the boys, signed nothing, and Derek Forsyth became distinctly jittery about the legal consequences. He thought nervously of million dollar lawsuits for invasion of privacy, of awful consequences if one of the girls was under legal age. He went to a lawyer.

'The lawyer's advice,' Peccinotti reports, 'was that we shouldn't be doing it.'

There was an escape clause, however, and it lay in Peccinotti's original idea. The calendar was not being sold, and nothing was set up for it – the girl reading *Last Exit To Brooklyn* really was; and reportage can be done without the subject's permission. 'We weren't suggesting anything,' Peccinotti says, 'and so we might be all right.'

His pictures became a black-framed montage of visible, surfside Californian life – then still a fantasy for Europeans, since the 747 had not yet brought cheap transatlantic fares. They work through the contrast – on one hand, the model in a 69 football shirt, with an obvious double sense, and the mouth pictures; on the other, the outdoor, everyday life of beach and freeway. The original notion had not worked. But the pictures did.

And working without models did at least confirm his prejudices. 'Models are pretty, they have good figures, they are nice people,' Peccinotti says. 'Models really are the ideal props.'

California, 1969. The Classic
Cat strip club on Sunset Strip
where housewives and secretaries
took their clothes off and Peccinotti
caught them for the calendar.

Unlike the girls in the beach
photographs, who were amateurs,
these models were paid to show
symbols of American life: Coca-Cola,
ice popsicles, gum, cigarettes. These
shots have the potency of dreams.
Remember, the West Coast was then
beyond the reach of most Britishers.

The Classic Cat, Sunset Strip.
Strippers for the fun of it.

Lovely – and they know it. Malibu
beach was thronging with gorgeous
girls, and gave more than a hint
of abandon.

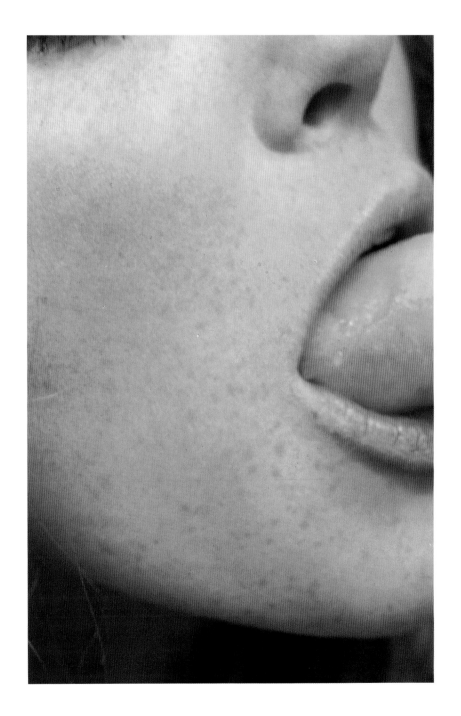

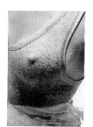

# 1970: Francis Giacobetti in the Bahamas

'I was for woman a kind of specialist,' Francis Giacobetti says, 'and why not? I am still a specialist, but an old one; I'm just a technician now.'

Giacobetti's nudes had made him the philosopher, and the main purveyor, of a kind of glamour – dramatic, with a perfect sheen, and a strong reek of sexuality; any calendar he made would be lush with boiling skies and crystal seas, and women who sensed the glory of their bodies. His graphic sense, and his taste for romance had taken him far from the simple and the natural; Derek Forsyth was art directing and creating the calendar alone for the first time, and he wanted just that grand sense of drama.

Giacobetti had helped found *Lui*, the French men's magazine, and he was a consultant for *Playboy*; aside from his fashion and advertising work, he saw all the variations that the new openness allowed. 'The girls in *Playboy*,' he says, 'are like Barbie dolls, always, and with huge breasts which is what the Americans love. Everything was planned; Hefner wrote the Bible and when you wanted to shoot a girl against a pink background, they'd reach for the Book and tell you Hefner said on 23 October 1965 you must never put a girl against pink. They didn't know why, but Hefner said so. The magazine was not very serious, but the people who made it were.

> *'We didn't have the girl next door. We took girls all over the world and made fantasies. We just did graphic things on a beach. I am a voyeur; the pleasure is to look.'*

'On *Lui* we were three friends working together – we could shoot an issue in a week, where *Playboy* spent a month on a centrefold. We didn't have the girl next door. We took girls all over the world and we made fantasies. To us, if a high society girl shows her body, that excites us; when it's some tramp, it just seems normal. We dressed the girls as if they were very elegant – very Hermès, very Louis Vuitton (at the time – now Vuitton is for the Japanese). It was a great success, but now it's kitsch.'

Giacobetti knew the perfect crystalline seas around the Bahamas from fashion pictures he had made for *Nova*; he was happy to go back. The brief was simply women, and his own very sharp eye. 'We just did graphic things on a beach,' he says. 'Derek and I were graphics snobs, for which I respect him very much, but we didn't set out to do something very sexy. That was not our cup of tea.

'But we knew the real reason for the calendar was the garage and we were always talking about it – 'Maybe this isn't enough for the garage.' We never quite knew if it had to be this way for the garage, that way for the Pirelli top people, another for Derek or me.'

He always planned to dramatize sea and sky, sometimes setting a tiny girl against a tumult of clouds and a sparkle of water; everything was shot on a very wide angle lens, and through special filters which he had devised. The idea came from shooting through a girlfriend's sunglasses, but the plastic took away the sharpness Giacobetti treasures. He needed a degraded filter, which would darken the sky but not the foreground, and he found it in Hollywood; his images are possible because the boundary between still and movie technology – and thinking – was breaking down.

But the skies over Paradise Island were obstinately dull. Every day, there was the promise of better weather that somehow never arrived; it was soon too late to go elsewhere. 'The work was dangerous because you went off as if reporting, or for a fashion shoot for *Elle* or *Vogue*; if the weather isn't good, you have

problems. But you go because, however much you discuss the pictures beforehand between photographer and art director, you don't go out to remake what you've discussed, not for a Pirelli Calendar. If that was the way, I'd demand a studio.'

Giacobetti loved women, chased women, and they responded to the glamour photographers still had; but when working, he was detached. 'I never remember the girl's name,' he says. 'I always call her *chérie*, that way I have no problem. I hate to have twenty-five people around when I'm working, and if the boyfriend is there, the girl poses for him and not for me, but I'm not married to those girls. What matters is the job.

'The pleasure is shooting the pictures, not the result. In my whole career, I'm happy with maybe twenty pictures; but when I make the picture, even a bad picture, I'm happy. I'm like a fisherman when he is waiting for the fish. To shoot a girl, or to shoot a landscape, to me it's the same.

'I am a voyeur,' he says. 'The pleasure is to look.'

Not every woman responded; some found him gruff, remote and likely to be there with a camera quite unexpectedly, almost as

though he sneaked onto the beach, and stole a picture they had not meant to give.

Alexandra Bastedo arrived conditionally, a nice Hove girl with respectable parents (her own description) who thought of herself as an actress but also knew she made far, far more money as a model. She was a television star from a series called *The Champions*, and a poster girl across Europe; to put her in a calendar would intrigue the audience.

But she was sure, from the start, she would never wear less than a bikini; when she arrived, she hated the way Giacobetti was shooting portions of bodies and not her face ('which is my best

The Bahamas, 1970. At dawn Anak faces Giacobetti's lens and the discerning eye of Art Director Derek Forsyth.

feature') and she would not give all the poses that he wanted. 'They were tame by today's standards,' she says, 'but I thought they were suggestive. I disappointed him.'

It seems a very modern confrontation, a woman resisting a man's power to look at her and make her what he wants. 'It didn't take courage,' Bastedo says. 'It's easy to say no when you have a return ticket in your handbag.'

Giacobetti, of course, had other girls, enough to make a calendar that proved a sensation. Forsyth had encouraged him to stretch technique, and then presented huge pictures, beautifully produced. The trade approved; but so, too, did the public.

A graphic way of telling the customer where it was this year – the original idea for the calendar cover.

Paula Martine. A sub-tropical haze suffuses this photograph, and seems to subdue the girl . . . Not used.

A sensuous photograph
and a painstaking shot.
Paula Martine.

Freedom within a graphic
discipline – horizontals and
verticals. Paula Martine
again. Giacobetti did wonders
for the sky.

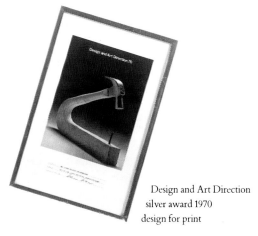

Design and Art Direction
silver award 1970
design for print

These cunningly conceived
stills suggest motion – a
rocking to and fro?
Coarse sand, skin, flowers and
fruit conspire with the sun.
Paula Martine.

Paula Martine

Paula Martine

Paula Martine

Paula Martine

Anak

Alexandra Bastedo

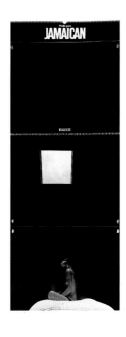

# 1971: Francis Giacobetti in Jamaica

The elegance of Francis Giacobetti's pictures is also an elegance of body – the sleek, perfected limbs of fashion models, their grace and also their ability to hold the camera's attention. There were few London models prepared to take off their clothes for published pictures, and both skilled and lovely enough to make the pictures work; even in 1970, that was risky work. Kate Howard did it, but just before she left for Jamaica she had appeared in posters for the *Daily Mail* – a bare back view, which now would seem quite innocent. When David Frost unfurled the poster on TV, half the studio audience called it obscene.

Despite this, Derek Forsyth still cast Kate Howard for the Pirelli Calendar; the problem was the blonde. Bo Baker was hired, blonde alright, but only sixteen, and Giacobetti's office could not tell the Bow Street Magistrates exactly where she would stay in Jamaica and the name of a chaperone; Bo stayed at home because the magistrates had 'insufficient information'. The night before leaving for the Caribbean, Giacobetti had dinner with Forsyth at Meridiana on the Fulham Road, and teased him about the British blonde crisis.

*There were few London models prepared to take off their clothes for published pictures. 'Glamour is very close to pornography . . .'*

Perhaps, he said, Sicilian genes had taken over Britain, and the whole race had dark eyes and black hair. This was a dig at Forsyth, whose wife is Sicilian. But perhaps that girl walking back to her table might be a model? 'What can I do?' Forsyth moaned. She was blonde, though.

He summoned up his courage and crossed to the table where she was sitting with Roman Polanski and her actor boyfriend; and Derek asked if she would come, tomorrow, to Jamaica. She had the cool of her eighteen years; she said she'd think about it. She was on the island a few days later.

Like the others, she came to a grand plantation house, a sprawl of colonial memories in stone; there was a reception line of curtseying servants to greet them, and four poster beds under veils of thick mosquito netting, and a vast dining room with maids whose giggles suggested ganja. There was also a private beach for removing unsightly lines of white from English bodies; the neighbours were not happy at the nude swimming, and the estate agent, a lord who lived on Pineapple Place in Ochos Rios, complained that he found himself 'walking on dangerous ground'.

'The girls were alone,' Giacobetti remembers, 'and they were lost and the atmosphere was very strange. We always heard noises; someone went down to get water and you would open your door and see a woman walking in the corridor, nude. After sunset, it was like living in a British movie.' The women dressed for dinner in long, almost Victorian gowns that happened, artfully, to be a little transparent. At night, the mosquito nets made the beds almost too hot for sleep, and the house stayed edgily awake. Kate Howard kept her door shut so as not to see who was creeping where.

'One day there was a huge storm and all the lights went out,' Giacobetti remembers. 'We were ten kilometres away in a kind of native ballroom, and one girl was sick, the youngest one. I took her back to the house and everything was black, no light at all, and the girl was afraid and so was I. I was acting macho, but I was afraid.

She went to take a shower and I was waiting on her bed, and I heard a noise I will remember all my life; a terrible scream – Ouaaaah!'

Giacobetti ran through the moonlit house to the shower. There, by the door, was the girl, and ahead of her, an enormous coconut crab. 'I do not have a sweet feeling about that place,' he says. 'It was very beautiful until nightfall, but it was *angoissant*, disturbing.'

Something of that feeling is in the pictures – the raw walls, the

woman on hands and knees under a great moon, the paraphernalia of the house's past. Sometimes Giacobetti made dream-like pictures which Forsyth had to crop to suit a calendar; the naked girl under a sea-grape tree at sunset is part of a much larger image in which the great ball of the sun is going down mistily into the tree, and the girl is a sharp, stark detail under it. And sometimes he simply revelled in the sensuality of the place. Kate Howard remembers still the feel of the black sand that sifted through her robe as the sea outlined her body; the pleasure she felt is in the picture, graphically.

'But if you think too much about the graphics of a picture, you lose the sexiness,' Giacobetti says. 'Glamour is very close to pornography; the angle mustn't be too clever. Guccione is very astute about that in *Penthouse* because the pictures are almost amateur and the girls are not too good-looking; but they look exactly as if they had just finished making love. That's the best aphrodisiac; not rhino horn or Spanish fly, but a woman who is excited.'

The Giacobetti-Forsyth calendar was suitably launched to an eager

Press, with rum punch and girls in plantation dresses. The launch was so successful that Robert Newman sometimes let himself wonder if it was any longer worth actually printing the calendar when so many column inches came just from this event.

But this was also the year in which Pirelli, strapped for cash, played with the unhappy idea of selling the calendar – through a high street store, and also through a colour magazine. Neither worked, but it seems, in retrospect, a most perverse idea. The calendar would no longer be a gift that made people feel singular and important; it would simply be a free early copy of something everyone could have for cash. The Press coverage rested largely on scribes who shared their insiders' privilege with the world.

The calendar, in short, had become something extraordinary. But its success made it harder to devise the pictures to match its standing, pictures that were unusual and outside the rules. Forsyth looked again at the Jamaica pictures, they lacked that Twenties feeling that he originally planned; that started him thinking.

It was time to take chances.

Jamaica 1971.
She came, she was photographed,
and then she was sent home.
Gail Allen.

This shot almost stayed the
course. It was processed and
printed for the calendar
cover – but finally rejected.

Angela McDonald at proof
stage. Not used.

Kate Howard

Angela McDonald

Christine Townson
(the blonde who came a
few days later), now
married to George Lazenby
(the actor boyfriend), with
their children.

92

Left, Kate Howard revels
in sea and black sand.
Above, Kate Howard today.

Buccaneer coast.
Caileen Bell.

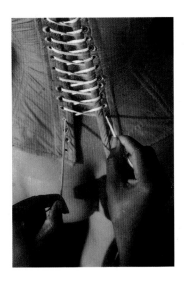

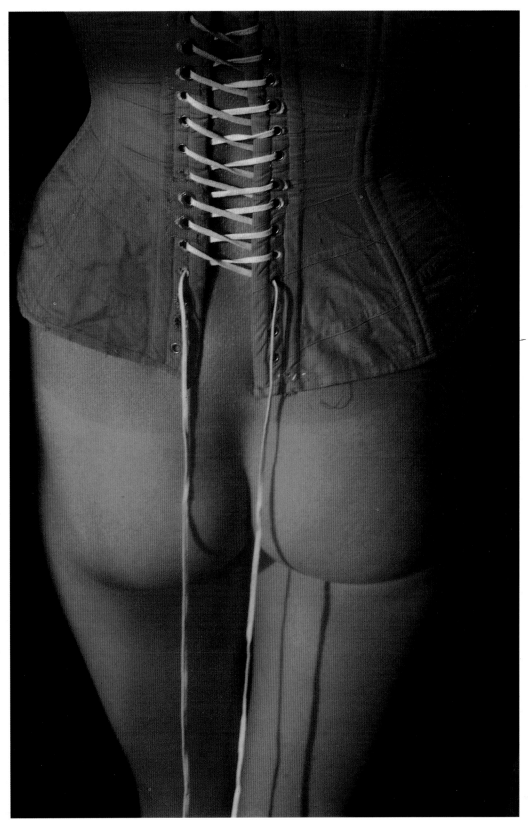

Kate Howard

Angela McDonald

Angela McDonald

Angela McDonald

Under a sea-grape tree
at sunset. Kate Howard.

# 4

## THE LOOK OF WOMAN

*. . . now anything goes,*
*nothing is easy*
*and glamour itself is in question;*
*is it patient lovers,*
*blatant pin-ups*
*or an unselfconscious intimacy?*

I t was the rules that made the Pirelli Calendar interesting in its first years – the rules that stopped a show of flesh and forced a subtler kind of story-telling, and suggestion. Now that anything was possible, nothing was easy.

By now the first Page Three girls were in the *Sun*, men's magazines spread women out like anatomical specimens; and Giacobetti had been responsible for the first nipple exposed in the calendar. Yet the Army had taken down the barrack room pin-ups, and Lord Longford was touring the sex shows and dirty book shops of Europe in order to save our souls. Soon it would be illegal to display indecent matter, and women wrapped themselves in layer after layer to make a shape that was only loosely natural. Derek Forsyth had to ask himself; what next?

'You reach a stage,' he mused, 'where all you can do is find bigger birds with bigger bosoms and smaller waists, which is a bore. Besides, the garage has become less important, so the calendar is aimed more at people who purchase tyres in large quantities.'

They had made the calendar a manifest success. It was 'the business gift par excellence', *Marketing* magazine said. 'It attracts attention, people use it, it keeps the name of the company in the recipient's eye all year and it spreads goodwill. It does all the things which business gifts so rarely do.' But the bills were paid in Britain, because it was still primarily a British phenomenon; only New York took a serious quantity, some three thousand from a print order of forty thousand; and Pirelli in Britain was worried enough about pennies to risk the calendar's security rather than pay for stamps to send it

out individually. Forsyth and Newman were grateful when schemes to sell the calendar collapsed; they were sure such ideas would kill the whole phenomenon within two years. In the bleak early Seventies, there was no prospect of an economic miracle to take away the pressure – there was a bitter miners' strike whose supporters tried to storm the Commons, a suggestion from Rothschilds that Britain would be one of Europe's poorest nations in fifteen years time and, at the end of 1973, the miserable, candlelit winter of three-day working weeks. The calendar was like a gaudy, glorious firework show on a cold autumn night, but it had to be justified.

Its subject was always women, but its reputation rested on wit, style, graphic elegance; orchestrated by Forsyth, the pictures were kept secret until the launch precisely because they were intended to be unexpected. It was left to other calendars to offer art without sex or sex without art. Moreover, the world's finest photographers were ready to make the calendar, because it was so much more than an assignment; the list for 1972 was dazzling, and even included the rather unlikely figure of Cecil Beaton.

*The first nipple exposed in the calendar . . . 'The business gift par excellence.'*

Derek Forsyth reasoned that his audience was exhausted by all the flesh and organs on offer elsewhere; it would be delighted by romance, a kinder sort of femininity. He chose a Paris photographer whose work was a kind of 35mm Impressionism, full of diffused light; far from the exact, sharply lit images of traditional glamour. More than that, the person he chose was a woman.

# 1972: Sarah Moon in Paris

Sarah Moon fools people. They take her reticence for lack of passion; they see a tiny woman and quite forget that, when she was a model, she could fill out an image. She chooses not to explain her work because she finds herself only repeating what other people say. When she was making her Pirelli Calendar, she would only scribble answers on journalists' questionnaires. 'What made her think she didn't want to be a model?' – 'Bored/time passing.' 'What put the camera idea into her head?' 'Camera took pictures.' They called her *moody*.

She used to have an assistant so trusted that often it was he who controlled the lighting and exposure while she operated the camera and directed the picture; onlookers sometimes missed the point of this collaboration, which was to put her own vision most exactly on to film. Almost nothing in her work is found or accidental – even the girl crossing a tideline of leaves on the calendar is a considered version of the many shoreline shots; even her reasons for working are deliberate. 'I don't go out into the street to take pictures; I need the assignment to do it. It would be ridiculous to create all this if nobody wanted it.'

In her 'applied work', which is often pictures to sell frocks or scents, she maintains a quality that is often called *painterly*. 'I used to mind the word,' she says, 'because photography and painting are so different for me. But I love the grain of film, and I still work with the grain; what I do now, though, is not so impressionistic.' She is individual, idiosyncratic, but paid for. 'Seduction is the limit,' she says, 'and it is what you must achieve. You have a very short time to succeed or miss, and you can't miss.' But simply making a product seductive does not make pictures. 'They also need what you believe in, what you think at the time.'

> **'You have a very short time to succeed or miss, and you can't miss.' (Sarah Moon). Her calendar had to evoke femininity.**

The quality of light in her pictures is unfamiliar – soft and broken. 'I was diffusing like mad – with Peter Stuyvesant paper, from the cigarette packets. I remember because Stanley Kubrick's assistant called to ask how I did my diffusion, and I don't think he believed me. Stuyvesant don't use the right paper any more; it's too thick.'

She was given no story for her calendar, just the subject: woman. 'It had to evoke femininity; the sex appeal could be discussed.' Moon likes to work in places she knows, with things she recognizes, and Derek Forsyth was happy enough to work in Paris – 'for reasons of economy and also to get away from the beach scenes,' as he told Pirelli's managing director.

Forsyth and his entourage went to the Villa les Tilleuls.

The house is in a Paris suburb, opposite the grand Chateau de Malmaison; it had lain derelict, without water or electricity, since the liberation of Paris, when the Gestapo, its last tenants, fled. The fine balcony no longer had all its pillars; there was the faint scuffling of rats in the leaves on the lawn; it was a place begging to be remade.

The walls had to be painted, the curtains hung, and Sarah Moon went to the flea markets, buying everything she liked – parasols and feather boas, a vast gramophone, bamboo screens, a piano and old photos of large women and whiskered labourers. 'It was like moving in,' she says, 'and that is why the pictures were so difficult to do at the beginning. I wanted to show off everything; the first pictures look like a decor job.'

Into this world, she brought women with whom she had worked before, who trusted her. 'It was summer and it was like being in a no man's land,' she says, 'just a place we had created. The sound was very important there; there was always one of the girls singing or playing the piano. They were doing nothing except waiting to be photographed.'

Some men were disturbed by the very idea that a woman had the authority to determine who looked at women, and how; they made up stories about Lesbian affairs and, when the calendar was finished, they said a house of women looked like some Lesbian's flat. In their nervousness at pictures that did not bear the usual labels of glamour – the smile, the eye contact, the sense of submission – they missed the point.

To the models, Sarah Moon was precise, but patient. 'A man, and the top ones at that, will keep you standing in awkward poses for hours on end,' Mick Lindburg says, 'but Sarah understands. She will tell you to go for a walk, lie down and relax and come back when you feel better.' Mick Lindburg at the time was a

wholesome cover for *Seventeen*, or a J.C. Penny catalogue; her agents hardly wanted her to grow up and take her clothes off. But she had worked with Moon before, and trusted her.

'Because,' Moon says, 'when you work for a man, it is a different dialogue. There is much more of a seduction; you work for the man looking at you. When you work for a woman you're in the same bag; it's much more a complicity. You don't have to be sexy all the time; you can be yourself.'

There was a summer languor about the shoot that masked the prodigiously hard work. Moon's models were, as Mick Lindburg remembers, mostly very small. 'You can imagine the troubles in making us all voluptuous; it was Hollywood make-up, glued and taped and painted. And they wanted us to be much fatter, so there were cakes and cream and *tartes aux pommes* by the dozen.' It sounds like a schoolgirl's idyll; Sarah Moon thinks that, possibly, Mick Lindburg simply liked to eat cake.

At night, Lindburg went to Pigalle to watch the working girls. It seemed to fit the story Sarah Moon, like a good director, had told her models – about New Orleans, and a *maison close,* not quite a bordello, where the girls would sing 'The House of the Rising Sun' at the piano; or else a group of women waiting for husbands or lovers to come back from war. 'Waiting,' she says, 'is the direction I give most – just wait!'

> *'When you work for a man, it is a different dialogue. There is much more of a seduction. When you work for a woman you don't have to be sexy all the time; you can be yourself.'*

'We became like *les girls*,' Suzanne Moncur remembers. 'We all knew each other's love stories. We felt like a family.' For Moncur, twenty-two years old and out of an unremarkable suburb of Detroit, there were pictures with expressions she had never seen on her own face, which showed a knowing maturity that had seemed very far away. 'I felt proud,' she says. 'Sarah showed me what I was going to be.'

All this had to be sold. On the last day of the shoot, when everyone was exhausted, the journalists came. One saw Sarah calling out instructions ('That's it, that's it!') across fifty metres to a model in a fine, old car – 'I was discovering long lenses then' – and wrote extensively about orgasms. The idea of a Sarah Moon calendar was intriguing, even odd, and it was tough to maintain anything like the usual Pirelli security. Agents talked, people speculated, and by

November the stiff memos were still circulating ('. . . essential that our Press guests are the first people outside Pirelli . . . to see the new edition.')

This time, the Press statements had to assert what men wanted, instead of taking it for granted. 'We believe,' Newman said, 'the modern male is bored with overexposure to nudity and secretly longs for the return of the fragile, ornate woman of the past.'
As Derek Forsyth argued, reasonably, the pictures were set in some period 'in which women were truly feminine – what could be more sexy than that?'
They were about to test the limits of the calendar.

Derek Forsyth, Mick Lindburg, Sarah Moon and her assistant prepare for the photograph in the garden of the *Villa les Tilleuls.*

Barbara Daly, make-up, prepares the models for the next picture.

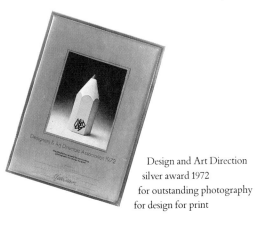

Design and Art Direction
silver award 1972
for outstanding photography
for design for print

THE PIRELLI
PIN-UP CALENDAR 1973

# 1973: Allen Jones with Philip Castle in London

The pin-up was more than mere kitsch to Allen Jones. In the early Sixties it presented a new possibility for representing the figure in art. He even gave lectures, with high seriousness, on the significance of Vargas as a watercolourist. The irony of this message within a Fine Art class was not lost on his students.

The vitality of images from the street abounded in his work. The shine on the heel and sheen on the leg became a trademark that can be seen in the Tate Gallery and other museums around the world, too numerous to mention.

He was an obvious candidate to make a calendar, if anyone had the courage to commission him. Jones was already controversial; he had become notorious for some sculptures that turned women into hatstands, or the crouching support of a coffee table. Whilst their boots and gloves were brilliant answers to the technical problems of the stylizing of feet and fingers in fibreglass, they also suggested the apparatus of odd sex. Jones could fill a gallery with other images, but somehow it was those sculptures that people remembered.

Derek Forsyth took the risk, and invited him. It was the first time that fine art had invaded the photographic world of the calendar, the first time a calendar would rest on the collaboration of at least three artists, only one of whom would, in ordinary circumstances, control the image – the painter, the photographer, and the airbrush artist who bridged the gap between the photograph and the images in Allen Jones' mind. 'It was,' Forsyth says, 'one of the most fraught assignments I was to do.'

Jones was not interested in executing twelve paintings for reproduction; with twelve paintings he could make a fine gallery show. What intrigued him was the possibility of manipulating processes available to him in his normal studio practice, to produce a unique product that could exist only as the calendar.

He needed a photographer to whom the technical problems of recording beautiful women would be routine, and an airbrush artist who could modify these images according to the artist's plan.

The first problem was to find a photographer inspired enough to make the pictures, and generous enough to give up control of the final result, as Jones says 'in which there was not a clash of egos.' The first attempt took alarmingly long and 'everyone looked like Baby Doll, without expressions', according to Forsyth. He had the uncomfortable job of finding a replacement and starting again. This time, he turned to Brian Duffy, whose 1965 calendar had been a huge success. The models included Jane Lumb (1964) and Pauline Stone (1965). Stone never did appear, because her husband, the actor Laurence Harvey, fell ill, but she did insist that Harvey approve her pose in a skin-tight suit of red rubber. He did, but only on the condition that he could keep the suit.

Allen Jones made sketches, while Duffy made the exceptional photographs. Philip Castle combined the two. Philip had discovered the airbrush at art school, from the fabulous sheen on car advertisements in 1950s American magazines. He loved the polish it gave, and he could never duplicate it with hand painting or pencil.

He was determined to raise the technique above a retoucher's method, meant just to tidy up the nudes in *Playboy* centrefolds or perfect the shine of some commercial wax; he had already made a famous poster of Elvis Presley, and produced the sinister posters for the movie *A Clockwork Orange*. The calendar – 'a lovely exercise', he says – allowed him for the first time to use the airbrush for fine art, not just the commercial work that paid his rent.

'Allen Jones virtually stood by me as I was working,' Castle says. He took enlarged prints, and traced Jones' sketches over Duffy's photographs – a marriage which required great tact. He then made a kind of jigsaw which allowed him to isolate each different patch of colour, and spray it separately. It was a long and painstaking job.

For a while it seemed the collaboration had gone well. But as the time for the calendar's launch came closer, Duffy demanded that his name be taken off his own fine pictures. He wrote sarcastically of his 'subservient and humble position', and he was acid about Jones' 'impartial and Godlike assessment of one's creative and original

*Jones was intrigued by the possibility of manipulating processes available to him to produce a unique product . . . the calendar.*

talent'. Duffy may not have realized what Jones had done once the photographs were made; he had seen only the thumbnail sketches and the end result. But he turned his anger on to the calendar itself. 'It's a pretentious load of old rubbish,' he told reporters. 'The pomposity of the Pirelli people is amazing. They're tit'n'ass pictures.'

There was even trouble when Derek Forsyth first showed the pictures

to Pirelli. Jones had drawn a girl at the edge of a billiard table, a red ball by her mouth; she sat very close to a pocket. As the picture appeared in the calendar, the pocket had been cropped out and we saw the whole girl, instead of an image which cuts through her face and seemed to invite us to lean towards her. The original concept can be seen in the sketch for the image.

And then, there was the ice-cream picture. It can sound innocuous; a woman had dropped ice-cream on to her half-bare breasts. Her brassière had been simplified with the airbrush; the picture was so closely cropped that it became quite arresting. Jones and Forsyth were summoned to Chester Square to explain the image to Pirelli's chairman, who was apparently worried that the picture looked like a pair of buttocks – 'which would,' Jones says, 'have been truly perverse.' On 27 October, for the first time in the calendar's history and only one month before the launch, the picture was banned.

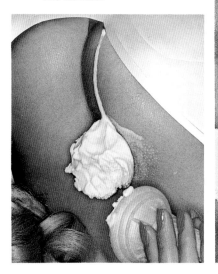

At short notice Jones had to substitute another idea. Ingenuity deserted him at this stage and he based the replacement on an illustration he had seen of a circus figure, a lusty dominating young woman in leather frills kneeling with a hoop.

The calendar was intended to be full of images that would not look out of place on the garage wall but which after a month of tea breaks might encourage an interested mechanic to reflect on the mechanics of 'seeing'.

A woman becomes what she wears, dissolving seamlessly into a tiger-stripe swimsuit or black rubber and high heels; Jones used rubber for its tactile quality which encouraged the eye of the beholder to caress the encased surface of the body 'as though with the hand'.

He also liked the material because in those days and perhaps so now, it was an anti-social material. Haute couture shunned it then, and Next has yet to embrace it. In the pictures bodies are tense, rather than abandoned: a model stands, back to us, arms out straight and head turned in a position that was anatomically impossible. So Philip Castle had to give her a new face. A model presses her hands against the frame of the picture, as if caught there. Another sits in red rubber; in Jones' drawing, she sits with her high-heeled feet pulled under her thighs in a way the model could not match.

Sometimes it is the whole image which is disconcerting. In January we look at a face in a mirror; below are splayed stockinged legs. The model has become the onlooker, the onlooker the model; the point of view has exploded. A woman wears a breastplate, literally in the form of breasts; but a breastplate is a part of male armour. Everything is as sharp and spotlit and carefully staged as theatre. 'If you even hope to try to establish some sort of presence that might have

anything like the shadow of the impact of a real person,' Jones says, 'you have to overstate.'

Some of the models remember discomfort, more than anything. Kate Howard was teetering on impossible heels, in acute discomfort. Jane Lumb is the secretary who sits at a glass table,

legs apart. She feels uneasy now about the way she's made to seem blatantly available. But there is a point to all this beyond the cheers of the garage hands and the dealers (and they *did* cheer). Allen Jones, with his background as a teacher, saw the calendar as a chance to turn the familiar conventions of the pin-up into a pictorial lesson.

The Marlborough gallery, Jones' dealers at that time, who represented artists such as Francis Bacon, Henry Moore and Sidney Nolan was mobbed by people fighting to get free calendars and champagne thoughtfully given away by the promoters. It was a riot of controversy. It was thought camp, perverse, brilliant; the owner of Atom Age, specialists in leather couture, asked for extra copies, and Forsyth was asked to send a copy to the House of Lords where Lord Longford was conducting his famous debate on pornography.

But the public arguments between Duffy and Jones, and the edge of

scandal at the launch, demanded some courage of Pirelli. Robert Newman had a perfect, quantifiable defence. He counted 121 press articles about the calendar, worth over £60,000 as advertising; he could remind his board that it was still tough for a car component firm to get its name into the unpaid columns of the press. More impressively, the public relations cost of the whole exercise was only £3,221. 'Our company,' he wrote, 'has a promotional vehicle unrivalled by our competitors, except the Goodyear airship Europa. However, the Europa cost £1.25 million to make . . .' But he knew he was fighting to keep the calendar alive.

Allen Jones

Philip Castle and family

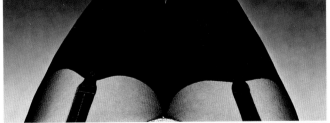

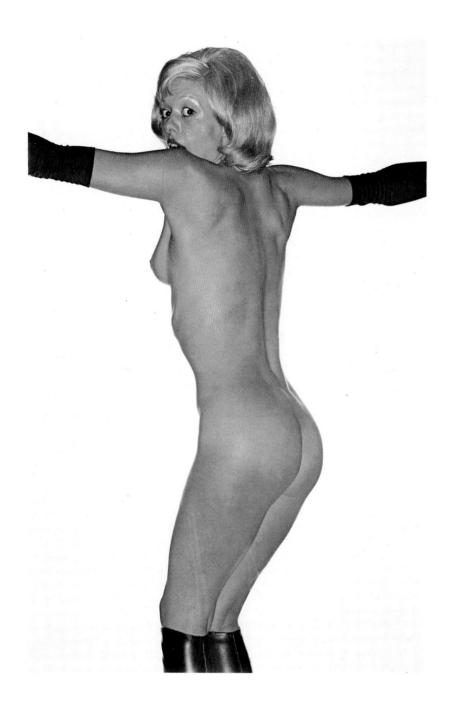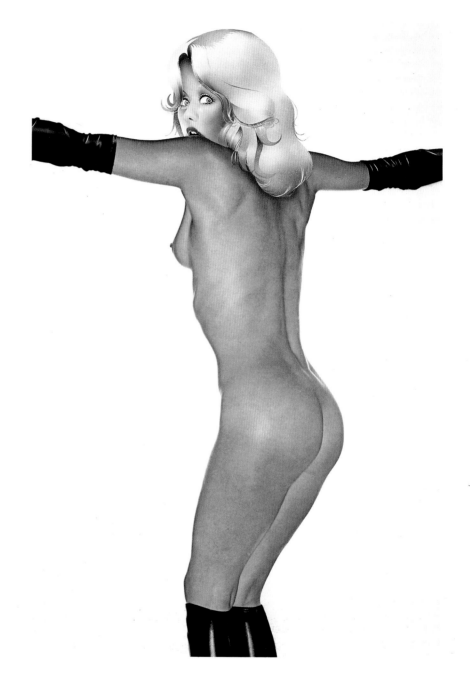

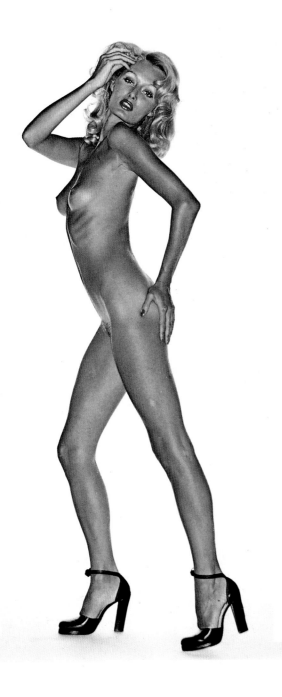

  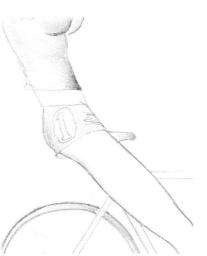

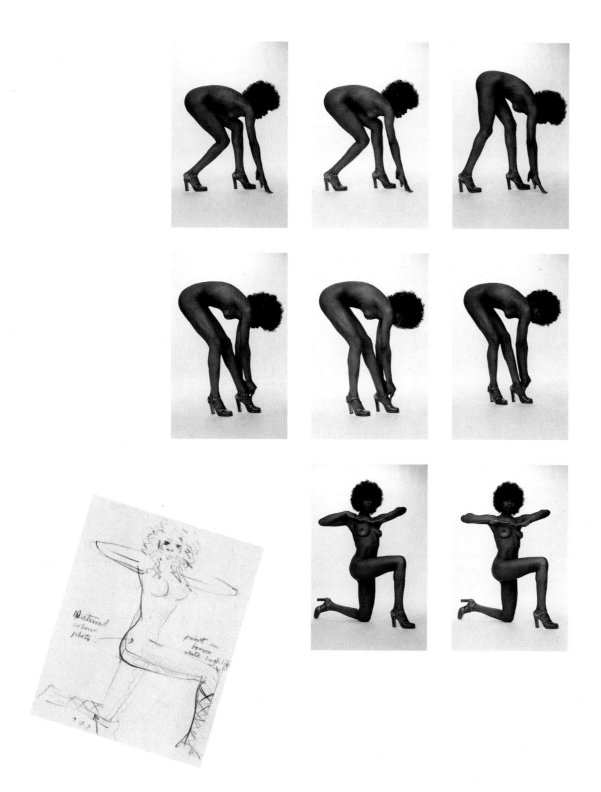

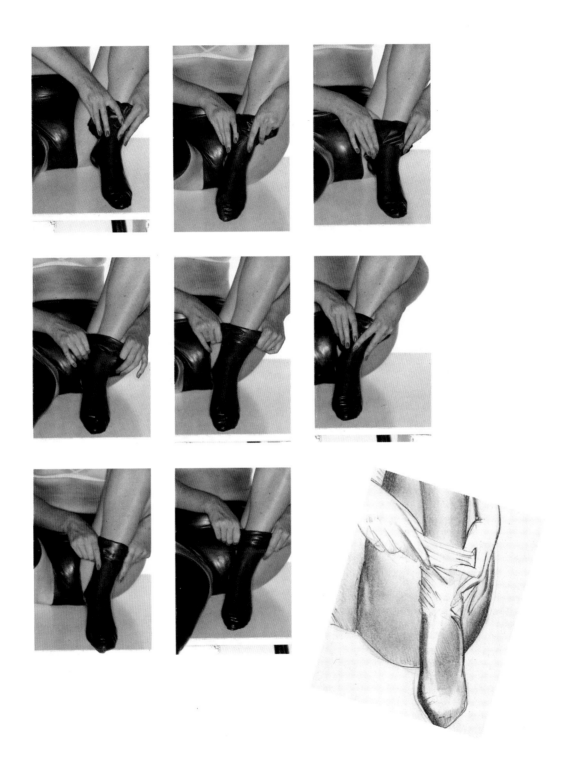

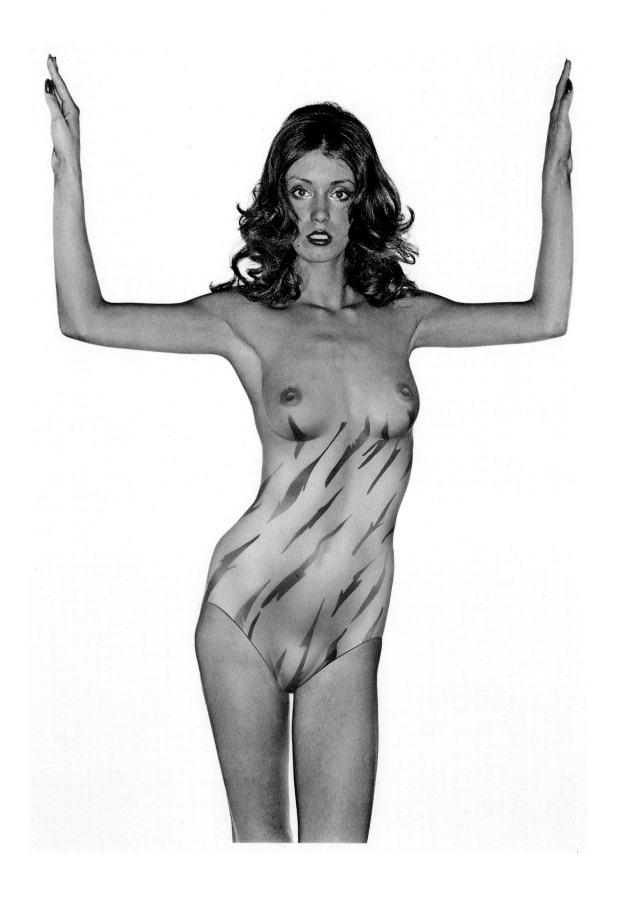

Design and Art Direction
silver award 1973
for outstanding photography
for design for print

# 1974: Hans Feurer in the Seychelles

Derek Forsyth thought of night and day, a trampoline, of models in 'a very male domain like lorry driving, eating, drinking, etcetera', alongside very powerful machinery, or 'in what is considered the most romantic, feminine place – like Tahiti, Bali or Japan'; or 'utilizing the cowboy and Indian theme, although this has been done'. He dreamed of a circus, and even found one in Miami. 'The female plays a large part in the circus and will have a strong visual effect.'

The calendar needed a lot of thought. The Sarah Moon calendar was criticized as 'too romantic and unsexy'. The Jones calendar seemed 'erotic and objectionable', a perverse document 'with appeal to the Press and the fringes of society', in the words of a company report. It was also the first time a picture Forsyth wanted had been banned, unlike the thirteenth and impossible image he often slipped to the board of directors, with some unacceptable detail, in order that they would more readily approve the other twelve.

*Feurer had his model leap again and again from under the waves until in one thousandth of a second, he caught the water on her . . .*

Pirelli's sales department had made it known they wanted pictures 'both human and realistic'. Forsyth insisted: 'I certainly do not think that the only way of achieving this is by going back to the beach.' The public and Press might love the calendar, but Pirelli had the kind of doubts which made Forsyth's position tricky.

At least he had his photographer – Hans Feurer, persuaded out of a most premature retirement. ('I got out of the business; I was farming in the Swiss mountains and philosophizing and so forth.') Feurer came from that generation of London art directors – like Peccinotti and Knapp – who turned photographer to put their ideas on film more precisely than others could.

When he agreed to make the calendar, he believed he was shooting a circus; but, at the start of May, Forsyth reluctantly abandoned the idea because it was proving too tricky to organize and too expensive. It was tough to train a fashion model to walk the high wire, or wrestle snakes, or even stay in the same cage with a lion. The calendar, it seemed, was suddenly without a concept.

They made a virtue of the fact. As Robert Newman explained to a magazine editor later that month: 'Their theme for next year is a particularly simple one, that of capturing sexily beauty and warmth . . .'

'Tit'n'ass, you can say' – Hans Feurer never did like fancy talk about his work. 'I like women,' he says, 'and I like to make images that you can look at for a long period, that aren't too definite; they can change meaning, give you new inspiration. If you see everything all at once it becomes boring.'

His pictures have a sense of intimacy that is very rare in nudes for the wall; they feel truly free, and not just licensed to expose more detail of the body. The photographer Barry Lategan, who later shot his own Pirelli Calendar, says: 'It's the uninhibited use of the body, rather than the body primed for the viewer. Feurer took away the keyhole aspect of it.'

The models were found mostly in Paris, not least to avoid the embarrassment of having them appear in some rival tyre company's calendar; and the team set out for the Seychelles. 'I have a tendency to look for isolated places,' Feurer says. 'The more isolated the better because I hate to be disturbed. I love the desert and the high mountains, far away places where everything becomes simplified.'

Derek Forsyth disconsolately adds: 'And where you have to catch your own lunch; Hans will never stay anywhere with hot water or electricity.'

With Feurer, you might think the calendar had gone back to its beginnings. He worked only with the vivid tropical light and almost always without filters (although that open red mouth dazzles because of a star filter).

At five each morning they would traipse down a mud track to the

sands and, from dawn to sunset, Feurer worked. For three days, he took no pictures at all, simply looking at the girls and the location; and then he began to shoot.

His concentration is fierce; the models who were not working were left to fuss and laze and grow discontented. Eva Nielsen tried to bury herself in her Ray Bradbury stories, but she still complained: 'There's a lot of jealousy and they behave like

spoiled children.' Chichinou snapped back: 'Perhaps we are, if those in charge behave like the parents of spoiled children.'

'The whole thing is like a circus,' Feurer said, sagely. 'But we are the ringmasters and we must make it work.'

His pictures work so well because they catch the one exceptional split-second in a situation which others might just stage and record; they work at the very limits of patience and technique. There are a thousand pictures of a girl in the sea, the water pouring over her, but Feurer had his model leap again and again from under the

waves until, in one thousandth of a second, he caught the water on her just like glass. Making such pictures could be punishing; for the picture of Eva Nielsen with a froth of toothpaste, Feurer had her clean her teeth for half an hour. 'It is not too bad,' she said, resignedly. 'My father was a dentist.'

More than most, it is a way of working which needs friends, or at least sympathizers; 'and some of the girls were pretty negative in their attitudes,' Feurer remembers. Two dared the tropical sun, despite warnings, and burned so badly they could not be photographed until the very end of the session; they were scarred and peeling, and therefore useless. Derek Forsyth's temper was short with them: 'I think they do it on purpose,' he said. 'It's the only way they can get attention.'

Derek Forsyth, Barbara Daly (Make-up) and models on their way to Praline Island.

When reporters and the TV crews arrived, the nervousness was set aside. Feurer staged shots for other people's cameras with a good grace, so that he could be sure his own work was not disturbed; the girls made centre spreads and prime-time television, and it was none of Feurer's concern that they could show only a substitute. The calendar seemed at its peak.

Hans Feurer

135

Marana

Kim and Marana

Kim, game for a planned pose.

Six shots from a thousand . . . each one thousandth of a second. The model has stamina; the photographer, patience.

Chichinou

Marana

Kim

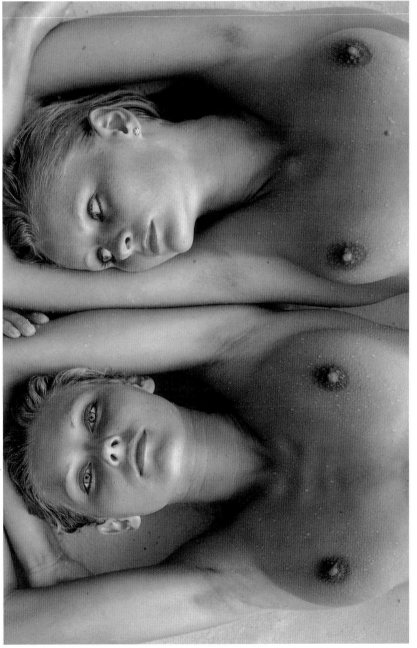

Kim and Eva Nielsen

Eva Nielsen

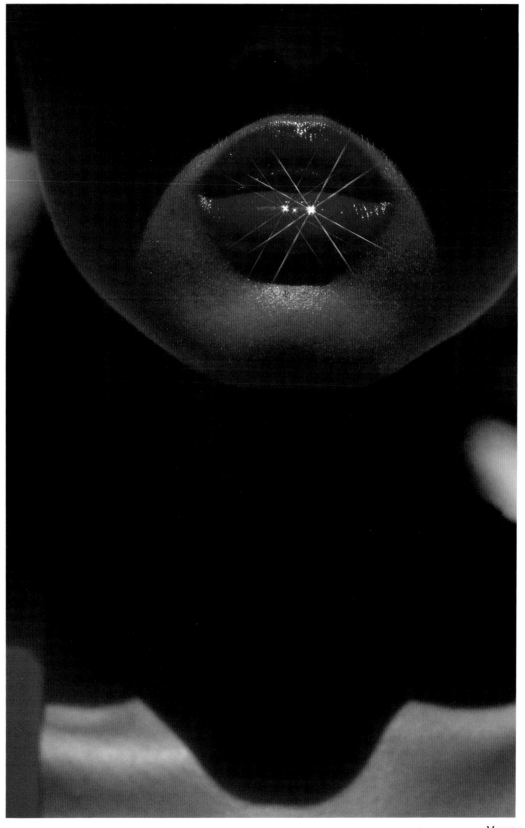

Marana

# INTERMISSION

*"We regret that, in the face of recent competition . . ."*

## GOODBYE TO ALL TH

By COLIN DUNNE

*Stars of a decade—in sand and silhouette*

*Tempted*

*Traded*

**A last, luscious leaf in the ten-year life of a super status symbol**

FOR the last time the sophisticated combination. These are the pin-ups for December 1974

*The vintage years . . . from the sunflower of '68 to the shadows, the stripes and the foaming finish of '74.*

END OF THE ROAD FOR A GLAMOROUS AND GLOSSY STATUS SYMBOL THAT SET OUT TO SELL TYRES WITH PHOTOS OF GIRLS, GIRLS, GIRLS

# Pirelli hang up their calendar

By BILL MARTIN

THE Pirelli calendar went to the wall yesterday. The tyre firm which created it decided to kill it off.

**Successful**

**Disappointed**

**1964** A pose for the first calendar by the girl who became Mrs Forsyth, the Italian model Marisa.

**1965** Showing a leg for prestige. The look cool. The model fully dressed. Others were not.

**1966** Something different for the times. The wet suit style. The zipper open. The glasses provocative.

**1968** The Sunflower. It's probably the least conventional of all the Pirelli photographs, nude or not.

**1969** Close-up on four faces. To some innocent and appealing. To others, they were something static.

**1970** The wet look. Actress Alexandra Bastedo doing her best to sell tyres from a Bahamas location.

**1971** On the beach. The arms folded. The expression wistful. Others more inviting and natural.

**1972** Model Inger Hammar in an outfit bought from the flea market. All girls were clothed this year.

**1973** Clothed from head to foot. Nudity no longer raising eyebrows in a permissive world?

**1974** The look for next month in what will be the last of the Pirelli calendars. For everybody who has always wanted one, is the page for April . . . your very mini Pirelli. It's your last chance outside the black market.

# The Intermission

A t nine a.m. on 27 March 1974, the story moved on the wires, a brief, cold end to a decade of celebration. The company language was flat as ice: Pirelli needed 'stronger means' of 'placing greater emphasis not only on our company name, but on those of our individual products in the market place'. The dream had been calculated out of existence.

There was outrage. The *Sun* put a fully dressed, middle-aged man on Page Three – Pirelli's managing director ('Oh, No, Antonio –He's

Fired Those Pirelli Pin-Ups'); the *Daily Mirror* was elegiac ('Goodbye To All This . . .'). Those who complained privately, from collectors and tyre dealers to zoology professors, were told the calendar had served its purpose, that 1974 had been the most successful edition ever – 'We should retire from the field whilst still at the top.' The protesters read on, bleakly unconvinced they would 'prefer to remember it for the phenomenon it was, rather than for it to end up as an over-exploited has-been'.

They suspected, rightly, that this was not the whole story.

Success helped kill the calendar, certainly. Pirelli's customers started to take it for granted, and it was far too public a triumph to be refused to any of them. Every motor trade company seemed to have its glossy girly calendar. Success made the lawyers' letters over the Allen Jones calendar a matter of public interest; it embarrassed a management already strained and pressured. It was remarkable to have Pirelli's views on modern sexuality splashed in the New York papers, but it might not be useful. Indeed Pirelli had a new partner in Britain, their old rivals Dunlop, who had a quite different style. They had never quite seen the point of the calendar's elegant balance between graphics and raunchiness. 'Our own calendars,' said a Dunlop spokesperson, 'aren't subtle. They're pretty blatant, actually.'

Luck has a way of running out in such circumstances. Pirelli had always refused the calendar pictures to *Playboy*, because of the magazine's unequivocally naked centrefolds; but now Hans Feurer's pictures appeared in a struggling Englishman's magazine called *Private Collection*. A rather literary glossy, it had suddenly decided that only a very explicit scruffiness ('Meet Bernice . . .') could save it from folding. It was embarrassing company for Pirelli, just as the

1974 calendar was being launched.

Worse, a faltering business needed a flashy sacrifice. Shareholders found the calendar an all too public luxury while losses were mounting in Italy and, in Britain, credit squeezes were forcing the life out of the profitable business of selling car owners their second

*Those who complained were told the calendar had served its purpose, that 1974 had been the most successful edition ever – 'We should retire from the field whilst still at the top.'*

and third sets of tyres. Industrial troubles, and the misery of the three day week, left nobody sure that any company could market its way out of trouble. When the 1974 calendar was launched, the Pirelli board already knew they could not pay their interest bill with their trading profits for 1973. It did not help that they had borrowed from head office in ironclad currencies like the Swiss franc, and were attempting to pay back in feeble pounds.

The same shipwreck faced the whole trade, not just Pirelli. Tyre prices shifted weekly, as though they were some raw commodity – coffee, say, or sugar. But Pirelli's product had to be manufactured, with fixed costs. The basic market was the manufacturers of cars, who could drive a hard bargain; the profit was made when car buyers came to replace those tyres, and the excellence of radial tyres delayed that moment. The better Pirelli's product, the less money it stood to make; quality and the bottom line were ominously opposed.

The calendar's creators also realized they might have been just too successful in selling the public the fascination, the exclusive nature of the calendar, without forcing home any message about tyres, slippers, cable or webbing. Market research suggested Pirelli was known for calendars, if anything. 'Maybe Pirelli should sell its

calendars,' said a spiteful columnist in the ad trade's magazine *Campaign*, 'and give the tyres away'.

They had one consolation: the calendar lived in memory as very few slogans or publicity devices do. It was sold at auction; its value for insurance purposes crept slowly upwards; a volume of the pictures became the most expensive, and one of the fastest-selling paperbacks of its time. Inside Pirelli, the calendar was like some undeveloped corporate asset – a bit of land that might some day be developed, a company shell into which a business could be put.

It was only a sideshow, in the circumstances. Pirelli divorced its British partner Dunlop, and had to repay the dowry – millions in loans and capital, which had to be found at a time when profits

*Pirelli was known for its calendars, if anything. 'Maybe Pirelli should sell its calendars.'*

were swamped by the interest bill; in 1981, the year the divorce became final, the group lost £12.5 million. Head office pumped cash into their bothersome British operation but, even so, shareholders' equity was a minus quantity in 1982. Pirelli UK's most valuable asset was £27 million in tax losses which would come in useful only if, and when, it again made money.

There was talk of drastic retrenchment. 'Almost everything was wrong,' says Sandro Veronesi, now managing director of Pirelli Ltd, 'but I would say the attitude of top management most of all – the structure was all centralized, the factories had accountability but no authority.' Veronesi was then in charge of manufacturing, and he had just two weeks to put together a plan to save at least £5 million in two years. The aim was not efficiency, but survival.

It was a time for either the greatest caution, or the grandest gesture.

Massimo Moro, then the new managing director, chose the gesture.

'I admire the way he did it,' Veronesi says, 'without informing anybody in Italy. The company was still in a very bad situation. He was confident, of course, that things were going to get better by the time the calendar was ready.'

Moro set aside cash for a calendar in the late months of 1982, when the annual budget was being prepared. He did so at the urging of his marketing director, Martin Wood, who saw how the calendar might develop 'the latent image of a rather sexy, macho, performance Italian operation.'

Wood also understood there was some urgency. 'Enough time had passed for the first reissue to work,' he says, 'but I felt if we left it too long we would lose a generation. People who saw the old calendars were now 35 to 40, but there was a new generation – the 18 to 20 years olds who are an important part of everyone's market – who wouldn't know what we were talking about. It was an extra expense, so it was a bold move, but it was also a way of saying – we are really serious, and we're here.'

Even after ten years, however, it was no easier to decide exactly what the calendar should be. 'The idea of using women to sell tyres was innovative twenty years ago,' Derek Forsyth was saying, 'but it's

*A high erotic content meant that, while everyone remembered the frisson, only sixty-seven per cent could name the product. The calendar had to be calculated back, most carefully.*

become so commonplace nowadays that it's boring.' Other tyre companies proposed for 1984 the usual women, with the obligatory blonde, in Tahiti, the locker-room, the woods and (with Lichfield) Ibiza; and it was not obvious that nudes sold. Tests showed that advertisements with fully dressed women were remembered accurately by eighty-six per cent of those who saw them; but a high erotic content meant that, while everyone remembered the *frisson,* only sixty-seven per cent could name the product. The calendar had once been calculated out of existence; now it had to be calculated back, most carefully.

Milan was given little to wonder at; even the newest executives understood that the formal propriety of head office had once before kept the Pirelli name off a calendar. Inside the company, the news went out only to those who needed to know; and even they were not entirely sure they could afford to go ahead. The budget had been set in 1982, but the cheques for art director and photographer were not authorized until the beginning of June 1983. Even when the pictures were taken, the calendar designed and the launch date set, Pirelli executives were still exchanging anxious memos. The printing seemed excruciatingly slow; would there be copies for the launch? The calendar was supposed to sell tyres, and there was an acute shortage of tyres that autumn; should they, did they dare, go ahead?

A week before the launch, Massimo Moro told executives from Milan about the calendar; they were, at the time, in mid-air and on their way back from Scandinavia. It was much too late to have second thoughts.

The second act of the Pirelli Calendar drama opened on 14 October 1983, almost a decade after the cold announcement of its cancellation. At last Tom Northey, Pirelli's public relations manager in the UK, could tell his London colleagues that the curtain was about to go up. He sent them a simple telex: 'We are delighted to announce that the calendar is back.'

# 5

## IT'S BACK

*. . . not every national institution*
*comes back from the dead*
*with wit, style, class*
*and a fixed objective . . .*

There was a coach that morning to the Dorchester Hotel, from the Pirelli Social Club on the drab outskirts of Burton upon Trent, at 8.45 a.m. sharp. The massed executives had every reason to be smug and celebratory. They were going South to make sure people knew that the calendar was back, and the company and its confidence with it. Veronesi's two year plan had worked in one; the company's balance sheet was no longer an abomination; it was time for a party.

The Press assembled at the Dorchester, took their Macon Villages and their Fleurie, and applauded. 'It was a bomb,' says Sandro Veronesi. 'We had such a tremendous coverage from all the Press, we had the front cover of the *Sunday Times* magazine, we had it on TV. It was a kind of *festa*. The impact was so strong that nobody could object to the decision four months before.'

The calendar had changed, of course. You could have one for buying two tyres and sending in a coupon, a device that let Pirelli, for the first time, identify their customers and talk to them later. It was no longer a simple matter of getting attention and making friends. Instead, there was a clear objective – 'to promote the sale of all Pirelli brand tyres in the period mid-October 1983 to mid-February 1984.'

Martyn Walsh, a graduate of Saatchi & Saatchi became the calendar's new producer. He quit to form his own agency. He was presenting credentials around town and when Pirelli agreed to listen, he remembered the calendar. 'Frankly, I was like anyone in that situation – throwing out things in the hope that one hook will catch. Luckily, it did.'

*He put what he wanted on paper – 'girls/avant-garde/style . . . the escapist element.' He also wanted – and so did Pirelli – to focus the calendar on the Pirelli tyre.*

He put what he wanted on paper – 'girls/avant-garde/style . . . location as well as the sexuality must add to the escapist element.' But he also wanted – and so did Pirelli – to focus the calendar, for the first time, on the Pirelli *tyre*. He needed to reach the men, aged 25 to 35, who were likely to buy the performance tyres on which Pirelli's new success rested. He also needed the new generation of dealers, who ran tyre shops rather than racks on garage forecourts (and who also liked women). Soon, they would be offered tyres at fixed prices, an innovation for the trade, and their loyalty to a brand would matter more than ever.

From brief to launch, Walsh had four short months. He had never cast a calendar before; now he was confronted by a sea of possible flesh in Islington, and forced to eliminate more than a hundred bodies in a day. 'They all looked terrific in profile, but there are not that many who look really good in virtually any position,' he says. The Page Three girls slipped out of their clothes quickly enough, but Tom Northey wanted no familiar bodies. 'I want virgins,' he said, 'I don't want anything second-hand.'

He also needed silence to give real impact to the calendar's return. In July the company announced that all non-Pirelli personnel would be asked to sign letters of secrecy. Martyn Walsh was going to the model agencies, unable to say what the job was, or for whom; suspicious agents knew all the other calendars had been cast in January or February, and most were already shot and edited.

'I said to them, look, I'm not about to run off with your girls. All I can ask you to do is trust me.'

JANUARY

FEBRUARY

MARCH

APRIL

MAY

JUNE

JULY

AUGUST

SEPTEMBER

OCTOBER

NOVEMBER

DECEMBER

THE PIRELLI CALENDAR 1984

JANUARY

# 1984: Uwe Ommer in the Bahamas

'We had an idea to sell, which is to show the tyre tread, and that makes it different still from the other calendars, which are basically just nice girls in a nice location. I think this is a more modern approach,' Uwe Ommer says.

Martyn Walsh chose Ommer as photographer because 'If I had to be in a trench with anybody, I would happily be with him. He always knows how to make his way out of problems, and then to embellish things. I knew he would enjoy the thrill that we were flying by the seat of our pants.'

It was a set of practical allies that went off to the Bahamas, to the Club Med on Eleuthera, one of the Family Islands. Ommer had worked furiously in New York until the shoot started; his contribution was to suggest a few girls who turned out to be too expensive. Martyn Walsh, in contrast, came with neat, strong drawings, his crew of models, and props that were almost as expensive – from the garment district of New York and the studios of Camden Town. He was about to discover if all that added up to a Pirelli Calendar.

*Each picture was planned around a tyre tread pattern – the product was now almost visible. Sometimes the tyre tread was a hammock . . . Sometimes it was a prop . . . The tread even appears on a diving board in the ocean . . .*

Each picture was planned around a tyre tread pattern – the P6; it would criss-cross the beach, the sea floor, a landscape of bottoms; the product, so carefully kept out of earlier calendars, was now almost visible. There was even a story, which the company were ordered to deny, that the subjects somehow reflected the jargon of the tyre trade ('We believe,' the agency advised the company, 'you should remain cool and inscrutable about what the images actually mean . . .').

'The drawings were very precise, and he came to see me over a weekend and we tried to find out how to do them,' says Ommer. 'Some were very tricky, like the woman at the waterline, and her shadow with the pattern of the tyre tread. There's always a big difference between drawing something and the actual shot.'

The point of the pictures was the problem; the tread, and the visual wit. The calendar's cover is two bottoms painted with the pattern, a make-up job that took hours. The models fretted as the make-up man worked on them, and once he had finished, they could not stand and could not walk until the shot was done. There are better months than August for the Bahamas; the heat and humidity did not help.

Sometimes the tyre tread was a hammock that was hung by wires above the sea, or laid over a woman lying belly-down on the beach; once, the models stood in the sea and Ommer's inspiration was to see them through the mesh of the net. The tread was painted on to a woman's body, the illusion of swimsuit with the flick of a painted strap over one shoulder (Allen Jones did a tiger woman on the same principle in 1973); it was imprinted in sand through cut-outs on which the girls first sat, and then moved with infinite care into their poses. It washed off, brushed off, spoiled when the women moved.

Sometimes it was a prop. Plastic tyre marks, a foot long, were glued and sprinkled with sand; but they floated with each wave and had to be filled with concrete. A woman's shadow was made with a flat,

Manhattan window dummy in perspex, and then the woman added in a different shot; the problem was how to prop up the  dummy without casting another, unwanted shadow. The tread even appears on a diving board in the ocean, as a woman dives. ('It could have been Leni Riefenstahl and Nuremberg,' Walsh says.)

The shoot depended on rigging and improvising and occasional rough carpentry. The Club Med handymen built that diving board and the great pontoons that, carefully laid, look like the tread of a giant tyre.

The curse of Eleuthera was mosquitoes, with their unfailing instinct for biting and blemishing just where graphic considerations, among others, require perfection. It was tough, too, for the models to learn diving in three weeks; only one managed, and the constant repetitions exhausted her in an hour.

But Ommer's eye for a graphic image – the old Pirelli tradition – triumphed in the end over the rush and the various adversities. The shoot also inspired him, in a most unlooked-for way. 'I made a very big discovery,' he says, 'I was working on the beach and some of these black girls were bathing out there; I got really distracted when I saw them, and they gave me the idea for a book of pictures of black women. That's my most important souvenir of the calendar.'

On 5 September, barely back from the Bahamas, the calendar was presented to Massimo Moro (its name now, on memos, was P-Cal);

Moro approved. Some Pirelli divisions, however, did not. The furniture webbing company, for example, rather sniffily ordered only one hundred because 'the calendar was designed with Tyre Division's customers in mind.' And three weeks later, on 28 September, the calendar's future was put in doubt again. There was clearly going to be a shortage of tyres in the last part of 1983, although the supply position could change. 'If we do not have the tyres,' Martin Wood wrote, 'I agree there is no point in promoting the calendar.' He was still unsure just how much impact the re-birth would have.

But the process was unstoppable. The *Sunday Times* had taken the pictures for its colour magazine. Italian magazines like *Europeo* cleared space for it; and after *Bild-Zeitung* broke the news the German offices of Pirelli were swamped with requests. In Britain, there were to be regional launches around the country as well as the grand event in London (which needed two security men simply to guard the gifts).

The tradition was revived; in a few years, it would make Pirelli well known to seventy per cent of their potential customers, compared with the third who knew the name in 1982. Some *The tradition was revived; in a few years, it would make Pirelli well known to seventy per cent of their potential customers, compared with the third who knew the name in 1982.* executives reckoned the revival itself was the best PR and that to continue would be an anti-climax. When asked about the next year's calendar in late October, Martin Wood said: 'We have not yet decided whether we should produce one.'

He knew Massimo Moro was determined to nurse the British company back to strength; Moro who had stalled and evaded and kept quiet to ensure the calendar went ahead despite the rivalry of other parts of the group. What nobody yet knew was that Moro, the keeper of secrets, was a sick man.

Martyn Walsh indicates to
Uwe Ommer where he wants the tyre
tread to lie across the girls'
bottoms. On right, Trisha, Uwe's
assistant, and René, the
make-up artist.

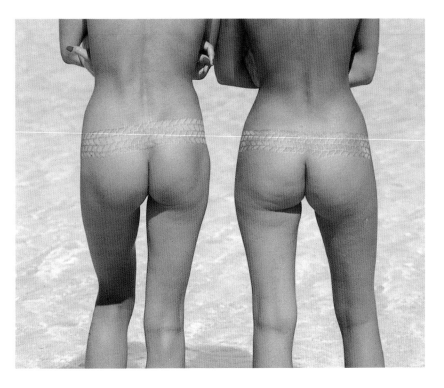

Julie Martin

Jane Wood

Angie Layne

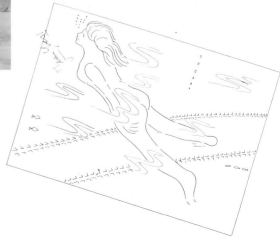

# 1985: Norman Parkinson in Edinburgh

At Christmas 1983, Moro called Sandro Veronesi. He asked if Sandro remembered the backache that had stopped his tennis and his jogging; he said the backache was cancer. He flew to Italy, went straight to a clinic near Milan, and never came back.

'I remember I used to go regularly to the hospital to talk to him,' Veronesi says. 'Even in the very last weeks, he wanted to be involved in the company. And he said, to a certain extent, let's exploit my position with headquarters, let's use this chance. They cannot say no to me, because I'm dying.'

Massimo Moro died on 2 June 1984; Veronesi keeps the date still in his diary. There followed an awkward interregnum all through the time the next calendar was being made.

The photographer was Norman Parkinson. 'Parks', an elegant Colonel figure, now in his seventies and distinguished, was the doyen of fashion photographers, trained in days when you took four sheets of film for three pages of a magazine (the fourth was for emergencies, in case the model moved). He learned how to shoot with a precision unknown to those who shoot and shoot on 35mm, finding the image in the darkroom rather than the viewfinder.

*'If I've had any success, it's because my photographs are really a portrait of the girl in the dress. She never has to look like a model . . .'*

He always wanted to do the Pirelli Calendar – 'because it's very difficult, the razor's edge.' He had tried a calendar already in 1984, for a cider firm, working with the Norwegian model Anna Andersen on beaches near his Tobago home, and with chain mail and arrows (the cider was called Strongbow). The calendar ran, oddly, from July to July and its release provoked tabloid copy about the Royal photographer and his nudes – 'What Would Ma'am Think?' The scandal upset both Pirelli and Parkinson; contracts were redrawn with clauses to stop 'salacious, domestically harmful or otherwise' comment.

For Parks himself sees little difference, for the photographer, between *Vogue* and the Pirelli Calendar. 'If I've had any success,' he says, 'it's because my photographs – particularly my fashion photographs – are really a portrait of the girl in the dress. She never has to look like a model; I choose the girls very carefully – there's nothing worse than seeing a girl in mink, and your first thought is that she must have earned it horizontally. Whatever situation we put a girl into, she really looks like she belongs – Daddy's paintings, her dogs, a small plane over Paris, whatever.

'The camera is only a gadget – the photographer uses it to show the way he thinks – his taste, his respect for women, his ability to have a girl move in a picture. The amateur is intimidated by the machine; he loses the pictures because he's still fiddling carefully with the numbers.'

Parks is vocal in his dislike for the men's magazine nudes that are full of gynaecological detail; 'What's blatant is a turn-off,' he says. 'You make love to a woman's mind much more than her body, or at least to what you find attractive about her which isn't her pubic hair. If you're a photographer and you respect women and you grow up with important models, you don't make passes at them – it soon breaks up your working relationship. It's not easy to take nudes in those circumstances; the ice gets a bit thin.'

It was proposed that the calendar should go backstage, to the *cabines* where models change for the catwalks of a Paris fashion show. It was territory Parks knew well – the shape of feet bent into too-small shoes, the bustle of crimpers and dressers and seamstresses, even girls who shout and scream when they're being zipped too tightly.

Walsh began to think about stockings, sweaters, furs, sequins, ties – natural ways in which the motif of the tyre trade could be used. He had, with great cunning and diplomacy, contrived that twelve London designers should, for once, co-operate; they would make a Pirelli collection, of shoes, hats, frocks and capes, all using the tread and not just, as one had suggested, to look as though a car had run over the hem of a dress.

Such a private fashion show needed a location; they found the Assembly Rooms in Edinburgh, a warren of grand, open rooms

***Clean is the word for the flesh tones; these are the impeccable bodies of the best models.*** under chandeliers and 'smaller rooms that were all painted in landlady cream with lots of ornamentation and fancy bits'. The models, international stars like Anna Andersen and Iman, left this provisional glitter every day to face the stalwart Edinburgh ladies in their felt hats, leaning into the wind. Smoke machines gave the catwalk a hazy glamour, but also brought the Edinburgh Fire Brigade. 'It seemed a surprising location,' Parks says.

The team lived together in a house outside the city, where the evenings were occupied in what Parks calls 'killer croquet – playing until the last light which made it so much easier to cheat.' The best

of models were prepared to take off their clothes for Norman Parkinson. 'I never realized how professional top models were,' Walsh says. 'Every morning they got up and exercised for at least an hour and a half.'

Parks aimed for 'perfect skin tones, with a full frontal, flatter sort of light which tells a slightly softer story'. The scuffed floors of the Assembly Rooms were covered in sailcloth obtained from a chandler, and the soft, grey-white reflection helped to light the flesh. 'Unless you light the nude with great care and delicacy,' he says, 'it looks like meat.'

He worked with cameras, Hasselblad or Polaroid, which made an exposure a full ten by eight inches. 'The larger the image, the better the reproduction when you want this quality of flesh tones,' he says. 'It's very difficult to get a good, clean enlargement from a 35mm picture – there just isn't enough emulsion on the film.'

Clean is the word both Walsh and Parkinson use for the quality of the flesh tones they wanted; these are the impeccable bodies of the best models, carefully maintained, intrinsically elegant. On these women, the *cache-sexe* looks correct, not euphemistic; Parks' parody of the Boucher painting of Miss O'Murphy, prone on a couch, matches the rather innocent eroticism of the original. There's nothing forced about the situations, although sometimes the garments were hard to integrate – one Japanese cloak, 'of the kind that leaves a woman looking like a half-tied parcel', according to Parkinson, simply had to be allowed to trail vaguely.

Parks works diligently but he also can work fast. That image for December – Anna Andersen and Iman tangled on a balustrade, with the fate of Iman's right leg still uncertain – was made in the mere fifteen minutes both stars could be together; one had to catch the plane on which the other had just arrived. It is a joky shot – two old friends clowning for the camera of a third, and wholly improvised.

Martyn Walsh had brief palpitations about its possible sexual innuendo, but then relaxed. 'It looks like a three legged starfish,' Parks points out. 'For me, it is just a nutty photograph,' says Walsh, 'but I remember going in to see Pirelli with some odd justifications like – well, this is the Christmas one, and anyway, at the end of

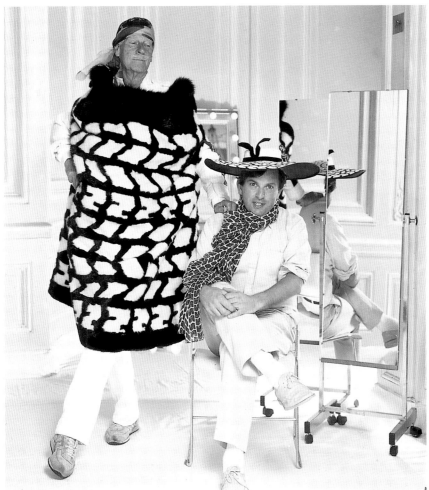

fashion shows they all drink champagne.'

Now the calendar was usually an honour to photographers, but in 1985 it was Norman Parkinson who provided the honour, giving the calendar (in the words of the *Sunday Times*) 'another hefty kick up the social staircase.' His calendar satisfied what some call the 'corrr!' audience; it was chic and well-connected; it justified a gala film and fashion show, an auction, a celebration.

But it looked rather different from Milan.

Norman Parkinson and Martyn Walsh off duty.

Patricia Roberts

Anna Andersen with Iman

Lena

Anna Andersen

Anna Andersen

Iman

# 1986: Bert Stern in the Cotswolds

It was only a question of priorities, according to Milan. In the rest of Europe, motor racing sold tyres; Pirelli UK would therefore not mind, would they, making a financial contribution towards Pirelli's Formula One activities?

The British company minded a great deal. The head of Pirelli's own tyre dealing company thought racing victories never did sell tyres in Britain – unlike Italy, France or South America: 'One can even argue,' he added, drily, 'that non-success is detrimental.' Besides, there was the question of the calendar, now such a tremendous success. Martin Wood told the new sales director, Peter Roberts: 'Clearly, for this sum, we shall have to abandon the calendar.' To his superiors, he wrote: 'Unless I am instructed to the contrary before 10 February, I will abandon the 1986 calendar.'

That year there was a great deal to abandon; the calendar had moved its furthest from being simply inspiration, girls and a beach. Walsh had already commissioned students at the Royal College of Art to paint pictures that included the P6 tyre tread, and a naked woman; he stayed unfazed when Pirelli changed the tread by

*Pirelli UK would not mind, would they, making a financial contribution towards Pirelli's Formula One activities? 'Clearly, for this sum, we shall have to abandon the calendar.'*

launching the P600 between the making of the paintings and the publication of the calendar. He had also invited Bert Stern, the man who made the last and perhaps the sweetest pictures of Marilyn Monroe, to make pictures of the students' art, and of the models – the artist's studio, and the artist's women, a thought as old as Paris postcards.

British Pirelli saved the calendar and helped establish that it was now an important part of Pirelli's public image around the world. For Bert Stern, it salvaged a rare assignment: where he could make commercial pictures for very personal reasons.

Stern had been an emperor of the image in Manhattan, with studios and a grand reputation that went worldwide with his pictures of Marilyn; for him, Marilyn was the best, a woman who moved and looked like no other. He chose, very suddenly, to quit his life in New York, ship all his possessions to Spain and make a new life; the decision started scandalous and untrue talk about his state of mind. Then, after months of exile, his work began to filter back, in Italian magazines at first. Martyn Walsh saw it, and decided to risk an invitation.

He brought Stern to an unlikely place: a Victorian woollen mill in the Cotswolds, a commercial cathedral whose open rooms could be lofts or studios or simply space with a wonderful summer light. ('The kind of garrets we think artists work in,' as Martyn Walsh says, 'except they all work in garages nowadays.') He offered a chance to work with works of art; Stern had sold pictures in New York, lunched with Warhol the day he was gunned down. The shoot was a grand return and Stern was even nervous about how he would react to working with naked women again. He was glad to find, when it started, that it was just work.

He admired the British models. 'In America this would be very difficult to do,' he says, 'because the good models wouldn't want to do pictures without their clothes on. You'd just get the riff-raff.' He also saw something darker – that British photographers had forgotten manners to their models, and that British models were more likely to do what they were told.

There was Samantha, for instance, terrified of snakes but cast as Medusa. Her furnace of red hair was threaded with plastic snakes, but they looked plastic; one at least had to be alive. Stern ignored her fears and went right up to the point where her panic showed. 'He is of the school,' Walsh says, 'who reckon the girls are there for the photographs.'

The shoot was tough enough for the girls, who had to be soaked with buckets of water, painted with eyes for nipples and trained on a trampoline for a leaping shot in which (after Salvador Dali) easel, model and the world seem to be jumping joyously together. But it was also a party – the dancing at night, the assistants making friends with the models (which is the assistants' privilege), the good wine Walsh provided for Stern ('who is a connoisseur,' he says, 'well, a wine snob, actually').

Stern does not analyse his methods, although he does say he was using a 6 by 7 format for the pictures, wide like the calendar itself; he thinks of his methods as 'magic'. But it was magic which required a great deal of calculation to bring together the paintings, the girls who were cast to look like them, and the kind of picture the calendar required.

His pictures seem like brilliant pastiche – a girl lies on her stomach, lit like *Playboy*; that athletic girl who's practised for days on her trampoline now springs into a white background, crisp like an Avedon advertisement; again and again, the blonde could almost be Marilyn. Look at the lips, the legs, the halo of hair on that woman who's looking into a camera; she is a wonderful physical presence

and she's preening, living through the camera. His cover girl purses her lips just like Marilyn. 'You see it,' Stern says, belligerently. 'I don't.'

But that cover is something different. The bare blonde, her dark glasses reflecting the pattern of the tyre tread, was technically difficult; Pirelli had tried in previous years to have the tyre tread reflected in glasses, and failed. But it is also an angry picture. It is, Stern says, exactly the cheesecake everyone expects; he's making fun of the bright white light around a glamour figure, the blonde disarray. It looks almost airbrushed, in the manner of those Japanese airbrush artists who can make you ersatz flesh or love; Stern thinks Marilyn Monroe was a victim of airbrushing in her last years, made into an artificial doll. He wanted to mock the techniques that spoiled her; it is the picture he loves best in the whole calendar.

Martyn Walsh left thinking of one other picture – a black model against an easel painting, the whole image grey-black except for a single outbreak of colour. It made him think thoughts about designer black, even black on black – a calendar, perhaps, where all the models were black. For once, the next idea had come quite easily.

The concept

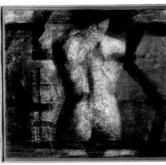
The painting

The result

Joni Flyn

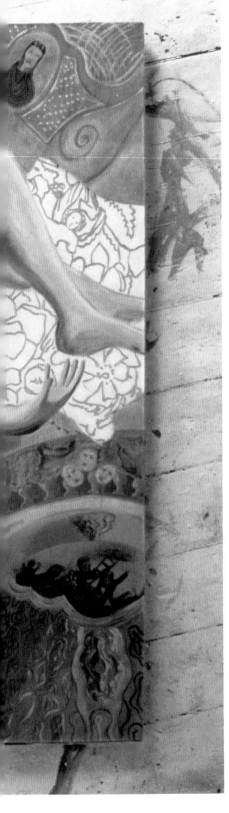

Jane Harwood

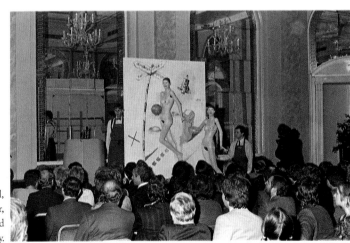

At the launch at the Café Royal,
London, the Duke of Westminster,
auctions the paintings in aid
of charity.

Beth Toussaint

Deborah Leng

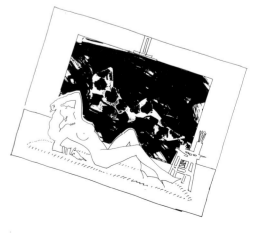

Samantha

Julia Boleno

# 1987: Terence Donovan in Bath

The tread of the tyre was a fixture now, something to ponder. Martyn Walsh came to think it looked like some natural thing – leaves, or the nets of colour on the skin of a snake; that led him to think of the bush, and coffee-coloured women who might all be from the same South American tribe. He thought of working in Brazil with maybe six black models, and the tyre tread shaped into the jewellery they wore.

When Martyn Walsh asked Terence Donovan where he wanted to shoot the 1987 calendar, Donovan says: 'I felt that the obsession with sand, sun and sea had been saturated by previous calendars. Therefore a simple, clean approach seemed more appropriate, based on the tactical assumption that when others are shouting, you must sometimes whisper to be heard.' The West Country seemed a surreal choice of location, but then Donovan has never resisted the surreal.

The fantasy of some distant Brazilian shoot was therefore soon changed to a simple backdrop in a studio somewhere in England. 'If we'd done it in Venezuela,' Donovan says, 'it would have been more ordinary.' The wonders of location are accidental, after all, and Donovan earns his fees by his skill in bringing together everything a picture needs at a fixed time, in a set place. 'I assemble all the things I like within twelve feet of where I'm standing, and then push and push until there's one simple thing that I find attractive. A lot of photographers try to get movement into photographs, which is perfectly all right, but I like what women look like.'

He has made commercials in Italy, shot fashion and politics (for the Christian Democrats) and he has two abiding impressions. 'If you go into a garage in Modena, the guy will have clean fingernails and the spanners will be very, very straight on the wall – Italians understand the look of things. They also love to operate in a ferment.'

In London, the brilliant black model is even more scarce than her white sister. After looking at three hundred girls, Donovan says 'you start looking at people walking down the street, but that's not a clever idea because, when you put them in front of a camera, they can't work out what they're doing there, wearing Tutankhamun's hat or whatever. Actresses, too, have great trouble doing it. That's the very interesting thing about models – they can get something going in their head and hold it until you capture it.'

*A simple, clean approach seemed more appropriate – you must sometimes whisper to be heard.*

For his backdrop, Donovan had put together fine clouds, for location he chose Bath. If that seems unlikely, it has to do with the sheer distance from London, and the daily round of his business and models' lives.

'You have to create a sort of vacuum,' says Donovan, 'and everyone is mustered there to get the job shot correctly; it is an atmosphere of mental cleanliness, if you like. I need it because I am convinced photography is a metaphysical process – what you see with your eyes through the back of the camera is definitely not what you get on the paper. That is the intrigue of it all.'

It was Donovan's idea that the calendar might be shot in black and white; 'Everybody who is visually sophisticated accepts that black and white is much smarter than colour. But I can never be responsible for other people's taste.' It crossed his mind that a corporation finds it hard to go monochrome; it looks as if they could not afford colour, even though the best black and white, exquisitely printed, is paradoxically as costly as the best colour. Instead he deliberately kept the colours as muted as possible.

Left to right:
Ioni Brown
Collette Brown
Naomi Campbell
Terence Donovan
Waris Dirie
Gillian de Turville
Martyn Walsh

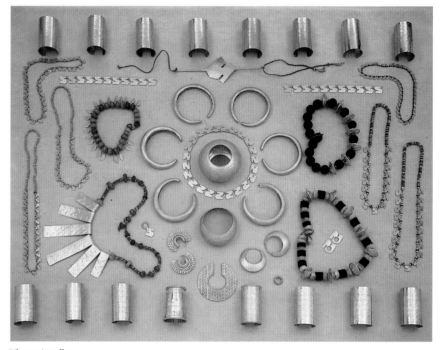

Pikuran jewellery
copied from that of the
Kirdi women of the Mandara
Mountains, Africa

# 1988: Barry Lategan with Gillian Lynne in London

The new calendar was advancing steadily through fashion, painting, jewellery; the arts had become part of the formula almost as surely as women and, now, the tyre tread. The next art, logically, would be dance.

It would be a celebration of more than bodies. Pirelli had come from catastrophe to a position close to market leader; the company had changed the tyre trade from a crude commodity business to a series of specialized products that motorists bothered to choose. The calendar itself had become an international institution, not confined to Britain; and its silver jubilee, its twenty-fifth birthday, was close.

Martyn Walsh had worked backstage when he was an art student and, by chance, he had met the choreographer Gillian Lynne through friends who auditioned for one of her shows; this was

*Lynne made a scenario on the seasons and the feelings they evoked – from the icicles of January, the biting February wind, the awakening of spring, to the warm glories of summer . . .*

before she helped reconstruct the British musical theatre with shows like *Cats* and *Phantom of the Opera*. He found her charming, and very unassuming. 'She was quite happy to come out with somebody who was a student who would buy her a half of bitter. You remember that. You think: she's approachable.'

He was sure that his new calendar would need a choreographer. He thought of enticing Nureyev from Paris, but it was always a wild dream; he went, instead, to Lynne.

Just improvising dance, with no story and no plans, could never work. Walsh had come up with a brief based on the four seasons (we drive, after all, twelve months of the year) and on the shift from one to the next. So Gillian Lynne made herself a scenario out of notes, month by month, on the seasons and the feelings they evoked – from the brittle icicles of January, bodies leaning against the biting February wind, the awakening and blossoming of spring ('in March I felt everybody was feeling sexy after winter, longing to feel free') to the warm glories of summer ('first touch, warm joy, propagating' for June). August was languid, fulfilled ('like after orgasm, darling,' she told the dancers) and November bleak, looking back at the lost summer; the year ends in the comfort, the burrowing hibernation of December.

And then, Lynne said she wanted a man. This man would not, strictly, be the first in the Pirelli Calendar; there had been surfers in the small frames of the Forsyth/Peccinotti calendar for 1969. But he would be the first designer man, deliberately there from the start. 'I didn't want to use him like a dancer,' Lynne says. 'I wanted to use him like a thing.' She'd use him as a constant so that dancers, and the audience's eye, had something to react against.

Now Gillian Lynne has worked in movies and in television; she understands very well how to compose for a frame. She was hired before a photographer was chosen for the 1988 calendar. That left uncertain the role of the figure who, usually, had been the star of the Pirelli Calendar.

'We were like sumo wrestlers,' Barry Lategan says, 'not hostile so much as each waiting for the other to make a move.' His first thought had been to make a black and white calendar, close to abstraction, from the stark tension in dancers' muscles. 'But since we had a choreographer,' he says, 'I realized I was going to have to produce a theatrical effect.'

Lategan lived with a dancer at one time, and used to spend his evenings in the wings and the boxes of the Royal Ballet; it was that electric time when Nureyev had just come to the West, and dancers like Fonteyn, Sibley, Dowell and Sleep were the new stars. Now he was quick to see the main problem. 'From a distance you don't hear the panting, or see the stress,' he says, 'but ballet dancers make a tremendous muscular effort that's transcended by the grace of what they do. If you freeze that grace, you see the tension – especially around the neck. And where previous calendars showed the girls' smooth bodies, ballet dancers are sinewy and muscular. Their bodies are white, not like the sun tan on the average tit'n'bum calendar.'

So the bodies were draped, and the faces disguised by metal masks, fashioned like the fenders and fins of cars, that made the classical dancers easier with the idea of being naked to the waist ('bloody chiffons,' Gillian Lynne came to consider some of the drapes, 'and if the helmets dropped a half inch in mid-*relevé*, the girls were totally blind.'). But Gillian had another idea – that there should be a man in the ballet. This chimed happily with the original proposal in which a male dancer was shown sheathed, skin-tight in the tyre tread pattern.

Lategan was reminded of his son's comics – Spiderman, in particular.

The viewpoint would be fixed; the viewer always has the same seat in the stalls. The stage would be wide and open, like the Kabuki stage that Lategan remembered, so he could show the entire body ('because ballet *is* the entire body'). He did everything to soften the line of strong, angular bodies; he insisted, for example, on ballet shoes. 'One girl was bleeding from some of the movements,' he remembered. 'Dancers' feet are subject to terrible strains.'

His cast came from the principals of the Royal Ballet and from the chorus lines of shows and musicals; Gillian Lynne's card index, from all her shows, was invaluable. 'How well they danced,' Lategan remembers, 'took precedence over how good their bodies were.' 'They had to be true to a line, true to the frame and true to their sexuality,' says Lynne, 'because I was making something that cloaks a great deal of sexuality. Not that I talked about that in front of the kids.'

They all assembled in a movie studio in the Old Kent Road. It helped that both Barry Lategan and Gillian Lynne work often in film, and know how to collaborate. It now became clear that the arabesque as a movement with its rise and fall of the dancers' bodies – caught at their zenith by Lategan – was to be a *leitmotiv* for this calendar to symbolize the turn of a wheel shod by Pirelli. The dance movement would be perfect, but some detail of a body

**Gillian's idea – that there should be a man in the ballet – chimed happily with Walsh.**

200

would be wrong for the camera and Barry Lategan would want it done again.

The transparencies were taken away to make a show of them, an elegant affair to be shown to the board and applauded; and then launched to the Press and the trade between the celebratory glasses of Buck's Fizz and the ballet commissioned for the occasion. The latest Pirelli Calendar was ready and waiting for its year.

Left to right, standing:
Chris Chapman, Kevin Iseley,
Gerry Judah, Helen Fitzwilliam,
Briony Brind, Sharon McGorian,
Kim Lonsdale, Hugo Bregman,
Nicola Keen, Victoria Dyer,
Carol Straker, Naomi Sorkin,
Mary Anando, Nick Clark,
Nadine Abensur, Diana Harvey.

Left to right, sitting:
Martyn Walsh, Gillian Lynne,
Anne Allen, Barry Lategan,
Caron Banfield, Cheryl Phelps.

Design sketch by Barry Lategan. This shows the inspiration for the dancer's costume masque – a motor-car mascot. It also shows the colour values that were being explored for the staging of the ballet, and the man's Spiderman costume. The sketch was one that was later used by Gerry Judah as a source of the making of the masks.

# The Photographers and other artists

**Derek Forsyth,** award-winning producer and designer of the Pirelli Calendar from 1964 to 1974, is one of Europe's leading industrial and commercial designers. From Art Editor of *Esquire*, he became publicity manager for Pirelli, launching the Cinturato tyre as brilliantly as the calendar. In 1969, he formed his own design consultancy whose clients include Rolls Royce, N.M. Rothschild, General Motors – and the Royal Family through the Royal Warranty. His first published book was the best-selling celebration of motor sport, *With Flying Colours* (1987).

**Robert Freeman** (1964) is an English photographer who has covered the world on editorial, advertising and corporate assignments. He made his name with a portrait of the Beatles in the year he made the Pirelli Calendar, and his work has been seen in major galleries in London, Paris, Melbourne and Tokyo; he has just finished a portrait of Brunei, commissioned by the Sultan, and is preparing books of his portraits of jazzmen and the Beatles, and his studies of Hong Kong.

**Brian Duffy** (1965, 1973) is the most publicity-shy of the London generation of the 1960s who put action into fashion pictures and made photography a fashionable career. He trained as a painter, became a fashion designer and antique dealer, and served his camera apprenticeship on *Vogue,* his work appeared in *Town* and *Elle* magazines and includes the gold surrealism of the first Benson and Hedges campaigns as well as movies like *Oh What A Lovely War,* which he produced.

**Peter Knapp** (1966) is a Swiss-born art director, painter and photographer who now art directs the French edition of *Fortune* magazine. He won an international reputation for his layouts in *Elle* and turned to fashion photography in the early 1960s; in 1966 he abandoned painting to concentrate on colour photography. He teaches at the *Academie Julian,* the Advanced School of Graphic Arts in Paris; his work has been shown in galleries throughout Europe and in the USA.

**Harri Peccinotti** (1968, 1969) is an art director and photographer for *Rolling Stone* magazine in Paris. Apart from two years  as a professional musician, he has worked in graphic design since the age of fourteen – designing record sleeves and working in

advertising before, in 1963, he designed and art directed *Nova* magazine. He has mixed design and photography for magazines that include *Twen, Vogue, Town, Elle* and *Queen,* winning many awards. He is now preparing a series of ethnic books and films.

**Francis Giacobetti** (1970, 1971) is based in Paris, and often works in Tokyo. He abandoned the study of law to be a photo-reporter for *Paris Match*, covering wars and stars, and later worked for *Life, Look, Nova* and *Twen.* His most significant client was *Lui*, the French men's magazine which he helped found in 1964. He has shot many advertising campaigns – notably for UTA – and his work has been shown in galleries from New York to Paris and Tokyo. In 1974, he directed a movie, *Emmanuelle II.*

**Sarah Moon** (1972) is a Paris-based photographer and film-maker whose career began on the other side of the camera, as a fashion model. Her radical images first came to notice in a 1968 avant-garde exhibition, Modinsolite; she was soon making pictures for Woolmark and, most famously, the designer Jean Cacherel. Her award-winning stills and films are in collections from the Paris *Bibliothèque Nationale* to the International Museum of Photography in Rochester, New York.

**Barbara Daly** (1972, 1973, 1974) is an internationally known make-up artist whose clients have included Jerry Hall, The Princess of Wales, Mrs Thatcher and Paul

McCartney. She trained with the BBC but left for the greater challenge of films and photography; she has worked for many international magazines, including *Vogue*; for photographers like Helmut Newton and Barry Lategan and on movies such as Stanley Kubrick's *Clockwork Orange* and *Barry Lyndon.* In 1986 she launched her own make-up range: Colourings.

**Philip Castle** (1973) is the British artist who, in the mid 1960s, rediscovered the airbrush as a creative tool in its own right. His commercial work includes a famous poster of Elvis Presley, covers for *Time* magazine and posters for movies like *Clockwork Orange*, and many advertisements for cars and airlines; he has worked for *Vogue, Elle* and many other fashion magazines. His more personal painting reflects an almost fanatical interest in flight, planes and flyers.

**Allen Jones R.A.** (1973) is the British artist whose calendar was bought for the Tate Gallery. He lives mainly in London, where he taught art in the 1960s and now maintains studios for both painting and sculpture; but he chooses to make most of his prints in the USA, from his base in Venice, California. His work is shown extensively in Britain and abroad, and is represented in many public and private collections throughout the world.

**Hans Feurer** (1974) is a leading photographer and art director who lives in Switzerland and, he says, hopes to die there. After a brilliant career in the 1960s on London magazines, he retired prematurely to farm and philosophize; it took the Pirelli calendar to end his retirement. Many critics agree that he is the finest glamour photographer in Europe, but perhaps, also, the least public man.

**Caroline Baker** (1974) is Fashion Editor of the London *Sunday Times,* and Contributing Fashion Editor to the Italian *Elle*. She was born in Argentina and worked as a secretary when she came to Britain in the 1960s – for Shirley Conran and for Molly Parkin, whom she succeeded as Fashion Editor of *Nova* magazine. She produced fashion pages for *Stern, Vogue, Elle* and the British edition of *Cosmopolitan* before joining the *Sunday Times* in 1986.

**Martyn Walsh** (Art Director of the Calendar 1984-) gave up dreams of following his father as a professional footballer to study graphics, and became the youngest Art Director at the equally young advertising agency of Doyle Dane Bernbach, where he created award-winning campaigns for Chivas Regal, Volkswagen and Christian Aid. In 1977, he joined Saatchi and Saatchi where his 1979 campaign for the Conservative Party – 'Labour isn't working' – won both awards and an election. In 1983, he was invited to re-launch the Pirelli Calendar; he has directed it for the past five years.

**Uwe Ommer** (1984) began his photographic career with a Grand Prix for youth photography which he won, aged eighteen, in his native Germany. He is now one of the world's top advertising photographers, with studios in both Paris and New York, and has a special interest in Africa, where he travels often. Among his three books is *African Sojourn*, a collection of portraits of black women introduced by the Senegalese poet Léopold Senghor.

**Norman Parkinson** (1985) is the doyen of British fashion photographers, who was apprenticed to Bond Street Court

photographers in the early 1930s. Within a few years, he was working for the main social and fashion magazines, and for many years he was the star of British *Vogue*; then, in the early 1960s, he joined *Queen* magazine and helped set a new style for glossy magazines. His generous portraits of Royalty and stars are as well-known as his fashion and advertising pictures.

**Bert Stern** (1986) is the only American photographer to make a Pirelli calendar. Since 1955, he has been among the world's top photographers – for *Vogue, Photo* and *Elle* and for advertising campaigns including the shots of the Great Pyramid upside down in a Martini Glass which launched Smirnoff Vodka in the U.S.A. His most famous model was Marilyn Monroe. He is preparing a major retrospective of his work for 1991, a book of his star portraits and an autobiography.

**Terence Donovan FRPS FRSA FIIP** (1987) took his first professional pictures aged 15; since then, he has visited some 72 countries taking pictures for magazines that include *Vogue, Elle, Marie Claire, Harpers & Queen* and *Cosmopolitan*. He has made more than 3,000 television commercials, produced dramas for American network TV and directed many pop videos including Robert Palmer's 'Addicted to Love' which was voted best male video of the year. He is also known for his Royal portraits.

**Barry Lategan** (1988) left his native South Africa to become an actor, but a meeting with the photographer Ginger Odes convinced him his camera hobby could become his profession. In London, he took the first pictures of Twiggy and worked for *Vogue*; his work has also appeared in *Elle, Marie Claire* and *Réalités*. Since 1977 he has divided his time between London and New York, directing TV commercials for women's products and fashion, and making fashion photographs.

**Gillian Lynne** (1988) is an internationally acclaimed director and choreographer, with more than thirty London and Broadway shows to her credit, including *The Phantom of the Opera* and *Cats*, for which she won an Olivier award and a Tony nomination. She has worked often for the Royal Opera House and the Royal Shakespeare Company and choreographed eleven major films including *Half A Sixpence, Man of La Mancha* and *Yentl*.